RACHEL SWABY *AND* KIT FOX

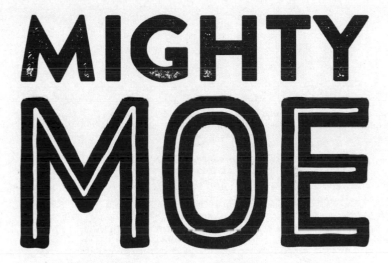

MIGHTY MOE

THE TRUE STORY OF A
Thirteen-Year-Old Women's
Running Revolutionary

Introduction by Kathrine Switzer
Afterword by Des Linden

Farrar Straus Giroux Books for Young Readers
An imprint of Macmillan Publishing Group, LLC
120 Broadway, New York, NY, 10271

Printed in the United States of America by LSC Communications,
Harrisonburg, Virginia
Designed by Monique Sterling
First edition, 2019
1   3   5   7   9   10   8   6   4   2

fiercereads.com

Library of Congress Cataloging-in-Publication Data

Names: Swaby, Rachel, author. | Fox, Kit (Christopher Swanson), author.
Title: Mighty Moe : the true story of a thirteen-year-old women's running revolutionary /
    Rachel Swaby and Kit Fox.
Description: First edition. | New York : Farrar Straus Giroux, 2019. | Audience: Ages: 10 to 16. |
    Includes bibliographical references and index.
Identifiers: LCCN 2019002264 | ISBN 9780374311605 (hardcover)
Subjects: LCSH: Wilton, Maureen, 1953—Juvenile literature. | Women long-distance runners—
    Canada—Biography—Juvenile literature. | Long-distance runners—Canada—Biography—
    Juvenile literature.
Classification: LCC GV1061.15.W54 S93 2019 | DDC 796.42092 [B]—dc23
LC record available at https://lccn.loc.gov/2019002264

Our books may be purchased in bulk for promotional, educational, or business use. Please
contact your local bookseller or the Macmillan Corporate and Premium Sales Department at
(800) 221-7945 ext. 5442 or by email at MacmillanSpecialMarkets@macmillan.com.

Photographs on page ii and in insert following page 208
are used courtesy of Maureen Mancuso, unless otherwise noted.

To Mom and Dad. Your love and support have made every good thing possible. —R.S.

To Mom and Pops, who taught me how to love to write—and run. —K.F.

And to Maureen, who taught us to run toward something great, even when the world tells us to run the other way.

CONTENTS

INTRODUCTION
Kathrine Switzer

Truth is always more amazing than fiction, and this story about Maureen Wilton is amazing. I'm happy to be a part of it, but at seventy-two I'm reminded yet again how weird it is to have events from more than fifty years ago spiral back into your life.

Imagine this: On April 19, 1967, when I was a twenty-year-old student at Syracuse University, I ran the Boston Marathon. I had officially registered for the race and ran wearing bib number 261. The race director saw me in the race and was infuriated by my presence in what he said was a "men's only" event. (There were no printed rules about this, by the way.) He jumped off the press bus, cursed, and— Well, you can read about what happened next in this book. Suffice it to say that after the race a huge dustup occurred: The official expelled me and my teammates from the AAU, the very rigid athletic federation that governed us then in sports. In those days, that usually meant the end of your career as an athlete.

A few days after our expulsion, I got a phone call from a guy in Canada inviting me and my team to come run a marathon in Toronto in just two weeks. He especially wanted me in the race because he wanted to enter a thirteen-year-old girl he was coaching whom he believed could run a world-record time. (The record then was 3:19:33.) My female presence would add "legitimacy" to the race for her, he said. I explained that I had blistered and bloody feet and could only jog slowly at best and would probably finish last, but he said that didn't matter. It was my physical presence that was needed.

Hey, we'd just been kicked out of running in the USA, and here was a country welcoming us with open arms! Like young American men avoiding the Vietnam War draft at the time, we burned our AAU cards and headed to Canada. And there I met Mighty Moe, Maureen Wilton: all eighty pounds of her.

She was very much a child and not a very happy-looking one, either. I couldn't help but wonder: *Does she want to do this or does her coach?* In any case, she ran like a pro, finished with a smile, and set a world's best of 3:15:23. Afterward she—the new world record holder!—told me she was more passionate about the rock band the Monkees than about running. I thought, *Uh-huh. Here today, gone tomorrow.*

For five hours in the car driving home after the race, we all talked about how talented kids often burn out; how at ages eleven to thirteen, kids have an ideal strength-to-height/weight ratio; how pushy parents and coaches usually break kids more than make them, etc. We agreed on two things: That this particular kid was an incredible runner. And that after age sixteen she would disappear and we'd never hear about Maureen Wilton again.

It turns out we were right, sort of.

Silence. For four decades.

Then, in 2009—forty-two years later—Moe and I had a chance to meet again. There she was, the same tiny thirteen-year-old, with a fifty-five-year-old face. I didn't know whether to laugh or cry. She had the same reaction. We hadn't been friends, we had only spoken on one occasion, and yet . . . and yet, we'd both been through a life-altering experience with running and it showed.

Running does that; in a sense, it both changes and chronicles our lives.

At our reunion we talked and talked. Mostly about the pressures we'd had on us for years. While mine involved controversies about women's rights in sports, hers were the memories of the assumptions outsiders made about her achievements and her career as a runner, including the notion that overbearing coaches and parents were abusing her by pushing her too hard, which was totally wrong. "I pushed myself, I was ambitious, and I looked unhappy when I ran because I was always running as hard as I could go! I realize now I didn't need to take it so seriously then. I made it hard."

Since my experience at Boston fifty-two years ago put me in the spotlight, I have dedicated my life to giving women around the globe an equal chance to run far and run fast. Moe, on the other hand, never got the credit she deserved for being the trailblazer that she is. Until now.

PROLOGUE

On April 13, 2003, a twenty-nine-year-old British phe nom named Paula Radcliffe flew through the streets of London, her two churning feet propelling her forward for 26.2 miles at a pace most of us could not keep up with if we were sprinting. She averaged 11.6 miles per hour—edging toward the speed limit for cars in residential neighborhoods. On TV stations broadcasting the race around the world, millions watched her take the lead of the London Marathon from the start. Thousands more witnessed her run in person. During the final mile (which she ran in roughly five minutes— more than twice as fast as the average female marathoner), cheering spectators pushed against the metal barricades, four, sometimes five rows deep.

Grimacing as she lifted her hands above her head, Paula charged through the finish line tape, then collapsed forward, grabbing her legs, utterly exhausted. She had shattered the women's marathon world record by more than two minutes with an astonishing time of two hours, fifteen minutes, and twenty-five seconds.

She was promptly rewarded with laurels and fanfare: $255,000 in prize money, an audience with British royals, interviews on morning and evening talk shows, household-name status for running fans around the globe.

It was an incredible athletic achievement—not to mention one of the most important moments in women's running. But none of it would have been possible if not for the grit and courage of a wiry thirteen-year-old Canadian girl from the suburbs of Toronto, Ontario, named Maureen Wilton.

Over the span of eighty-five years, an estimated twenty-six women besides Paula have had the singularly unique experience of standing at a finish line and realizing, *No other woman in the history of the world has completed 26.2 miles faster than me on foot.*

Some of those women were treated like Paula: They earned prize money, met world dignitaries, were greeted by screaming fans. But the further you jump back in time, the more underwhelming the reaction. Finish lines weren't filled with enthusiastic spectators or officials in suits holding ceremonial tape. Instead, there were blustering men, livid that *a woman* had the audacity to run a marathon. In other cases, hardly anyone watched at all.

Much of women's running history has been plagued by controversy, hate mail, and court cases. For decades, women were barred from running long distances. Some doctors spouted nonsense about running's dangers for a woman's health. They claimed the jostling from a running stride over several miles could damage a female's reproductive system and make her infertile.

Others believed running long distances simply wasn't feminine, that it was improper for women to sweat in public or do something so physically demanding. Those women who did run were ridiculed, often while they trained.

But slowly, attitudes changed. By 2010, more women were crossing finish lines than men. In 2016, more than seven million women participated in a road race, compared to just over five million men. That's because a group of brave rule-breakers—women who wanted to run fast and run far—forced their way into the sport, despite insults, public outcry, and defaming newspaper articles. They loved to run, and they weren't going to let any ill-informed doctor or race official stop them. So they revolted.

In 1963, Merry Lepper snuck to the starting line of the Western Hemisphere Marathon in California and finished, despite a race official who shouted that she'd never be able to have babies if she participated. At twenty, she became the first woman in America to finish an official marathon.

In 1966, Bobbi Gibb hid in the bushes near the

starting line of the Boston Marathon before joining the crowd of men after the race began. Though the Boston Marathon banned women's participation, she became the first woman to ever finish that race.

In 1967, Kathrine Switzer entered the Boston Marathon using the initials of her first and middle names. At the fourth mile, when a race director noticed a woman was on his course, he tried to tackle her. Kathrine and her boyfriend fended him off and she finished, the first woman to do so with an official bib.

In 1984, Joan Benoit Samuelson won the Olympic Marathon in Los Angeles. She was an American taking home gold in the first year that women were allowed to participate in the event at the Summer Games.

It's a heroic history, but for every women's running revolutionary we now celebrate, there are those we've forgotten.

PART I

THE RIBBON

1

The girl shouldn't be here.

Not on this dusty road north of Toronto, next to the fields filled with wildflowers and the newly constructed brick college buildings. Not alongside the twenty-eight men dressed in shorts and T-shirts and running shoes. The men are clustered away from the girl, stretching and shaking out their long arms and legs. They're tall, all of them towering like trees at least a foot above her. As they chatter and touch their knees to their chest, reach for their toes, or slowly jog in relaxed circles, the girl feels like she's standing on the edge of a forest.

On this late-spring Saturday morning, the girl should be at home, ten minutes down the 401 freeway, listening to her favorite records on the dresser-sized wood-paneled hi-fi stereo in her parents' living room. She should be lying on the rust-colored carpet, her hands clasping her chin as her foot taps to the beat of a song by the Monkees or the Beach Boys as she day-dreams about curling waves on a California beach.

Or she should be at the family property on Doe Lake, two hours north of here. By this point in the morning, she'd be in the water, cutting through the wake behind her parents' small aluminum motorboat on a slalom water ski. Or she'd be leaping off the giant rock out beyond the dock into the cold fresh water, trying to avoid getting splashed or dunked by her older brothers.

She should be riding her bike. She should be licking a chocolate-dipped cone from Dairy Queen. She should be doing homework, reading a book, or talking on the phone with a friend. She should be doing any one of the thousands of things a thirteen-year-old girl in 1967 from North York, Ontario, should be doing on a Saturday morning in May.

She's too short, too small, too young, and too, well, too much of a girl to be here.

Or at least that's what grown-ups have been saying for decades. In conference rooms and meeting halls and all the places where important adults—mostly men—decide official things about the sport of running. They declared that a girl should not be allowed to be here awaiting the start of this race with dozens of male contestants, a race that will go on for hours.

Actually, these official men haven't just decided that a girl like her shouldn't be allowed to try something like this. They've decided she couldn't do it even if they let her. It isn't possible. If she tried, they've proclaimed, it could damage her forever.

But the girl is still here—all four foot eight inches and eighty pounds of her—trying desperately not to catch the attention of the men as she ties her Puma shoes next to her mom's car.

Yes, the girl is here. And she is going to try to break a world record.

Though if you happened to be walking on Steeles Avenue in the Toronto suburb of North York, you wouldn't know a world-record attempt was about to happen. Which was strange. A world record is supposed to be momentous, historic. There's supposed to be fanfare and cameras and swelling crowds hoping to glimpse something that's never happened before.

Nine months earlier, three thousand miles southeast of here on a track at UC Berkeley in California, a University of Kansas student named Jim Ryun broke a world record, and he got all that. He ran a mile around a track in three minutes and fifty one seconds. Millions of people watched it on TV during ABC's *Wide World of Sports*; hundreds more witnessed it live. They screamed and clapped as Ryun's torso broke through a piece of string at the finish line.

There aren't any TV cameras here to broadcast the girl's record attempt. Just a few dozen people ambling around a registration table on the sidewalk. A wooden stake has been hammered into the grass. Stapled onto it is a small sign that reads MARATHON START in black handwritten letters.

The girl is standing off to the side with her mom. She is about to do, essentially, the same exact thing as Jim Ryun—run. But she's going to run thousands and thousands of steps farther than him—about fifty-two thousand to his two thousand. That means running for more than three hours, instead of more than three minutes.

Many of the grown men milling about in front of the starting line don't know she's going to do this. They are all listed on the event's program as official entrants in the Eastern Canadian Centennial Marathon Championships. Their names are on the second page in blue letters. There's Al Sinclaire and Wendon Adey, both from Gladstone. Jim Beisty and Herb Monck of Hamilton. There's Tom Miller and Tom Coulter from Syracuse, New York. There's more than twenty other names listed: all men who aren't afraid or nervous to be seen at a marathon starting line because they know they are allowed to be here.

The girl's name isn't listed with theirs. She's farther down the page, beneath the section that says "12:00 Noon: Women's Open 5 Miles." That, according to those official adult men in ties and blazers, is a respectable distance for someone like the girl. And so that is what the program says she is going to do: run five miles with twenty-two other women.

The marathon is scheduled to start five minutes before the women's race. "You need to get to the start line," the girl's mom says sternly, in the same tone of voice she uses when she tells the girl to clean her room.

But the girl isn't ready yet. She's nervous, and a little embarrassed. Not because she is about to run a marathon. She knows she can do that. She's been training for three years and knows what it feels like to run really long and really fast.

She's nervous what the men will think when she walks up to that starting line. *What will they say? What will they do?*

She inhales deeply. Then marches toward them.

As an experienced runner, she's completed a version of this routine hundreds of times before—the moments just before a race when everything seems quieter than it actually is, when you can hear your own heartbeat pulsing in your ears. It feels familiar in a way that helps her forget about those men and what they might say. *It's another race*, she thinks. *Just another race.*

She steps up toward the runners now gathering at the starting line. She jiggles her legs, shakes out her arms. She ignores the curious looks and smiles from some of the other participants.

"Runners, take your mark."

The girl takes a breath. *Relax. Relax.* It doesn't matter if she's not supposed to be here. She has a job to do. She has a record to break.

"Set."

Another breath. There's silence. The girl's muscles clench. She leans forward. Her fists are balled and her eyes are focused straight ahead.

Crack!

The sound of the starter's pistol pierces the air. The girl begins to run.

2

On November 30, 1953, the temperature in Toronto held just above freezing. Toronto Western Hospital, a tall brick building just over a mile north of Lake Ontario, stood among dull cloud cover. But inside the hospital, the weather didn't matter—not to Margaret and Roger Wilton. They were busy studying the folded legs, stretching fingers, and tiny, serious face of their newborn daughter.

Margaret Maureen Wilton was named after her mother, but they planned to call her by her middle name, Maureen. No one knew the way her life would shape the world just then. She was notable in the Wilton family because she was smaller than her two older siblings had been at birth, just five pounds, and a girl. A first for Margaret and Roger, who already had two boys, Gordon, six, and Dan, two and a half.

They brought Maureen home to a flat in the West End of Toronto. The Wilton family lived on one floor of an old brick house owned by Maureen's great-aunt. Maureen learned to crawl, walk, and run in this house. She danced through the kitchen and living room with her brothers and dressed up in cowboy hats. In the months without snow, Maureen charged around the uneven sidewalks on her metal tricycle and played with a boy next door. When the temperature plunged below freezing, Roger Wilton made a small ice rink in the backyard for the kids to play on.

Maureen was three when her father introduced her to the slick stage. Roger tied skates onto her toddler feet, put a hockey stick in her hands, and placed her on the ice. Maureen stood oh so still, smiling up tentatively at her father from the fuzzy oval of her snowsuit hood. Her brothers had already been through this initiation, and now Maureen had passed it. She may have been small and the only girl, but no one in her family ever judged her by a different set of standards. If her brothers played hockey in the backyard, she did, too. When they chased each other through the house, Maureen darted between them.

Before Maureen's fourth birthday, feeling the squeeze of three young children in a small flat in a tightly packed city neighborhood, her parents moved the family to Ajax. Ajax is now considered part of the Greater Toronto area, but at the time, it was a planned housing development plopped in the middle of farmland. When the Wiltons arrived, the community had just elected its first set of city officials.

The new neighborhood delighted Maureen. It was as if everything had opened up and spread out. There were no more tall buildings crowded onto one city block. Now, as she looked down her street, she saw unruly fields at the end of it. The grass waved in the prevailing winds from nearby Lake Ontario. Wide-open space was the only playground Maureen ever needed.

During the week, Maureen's father made the thirty-mile commute to Toronto each evening to work the night shift as a printer at Maclean Hunter. Maureen would see him in the mornings as he returned home from the magazine-publishing company. They'd chat as she ate a few spoonfuls of Cream of Wheat or cold cereal before school. And then, hair pulled up on each side with metal clips and wearing a dress her mother had ironed, Maureen bounced outside to claim a few minutes of freedom before class started.

When she got older, she found bliss furiously pedaling her bicycle. It felt good to ride fast, a way to get her energy out and open up her lungs. She zipped through the neighborhood on weekends and in the morning on the way to school. The first day the nuns saw her pull up to the bike rack in front of St. Bernadette Catholic grade school (the Canadian version of elementary school), they started to fuss.

"Oh, you're riding a boys' bike," they said, eyeing

the hand-me-down from her older brothers. The bike's battered frame had a horizontal top tube Maureen had to throw her leg over, which was different from girls' bikes, with a downward-slanting bar. Those were supposed to be easier to mount with a more "appropriate" leg maneuver.

The nuns smiled. Maureen knew they were impressed. She gave them a shy shrug and a little smile back and continued to her class.

Maureen enjoyed school and was fond of her new home, but nothing compared to her love for the family's annual summer trip to their lakefront property. Maureen would hop in the overloaded car with her brothers and parents and her cousin Tom, who often tagged along. They drove two hours north to a small marina on the shore of Doe Lake. There, they transferred all their clothes and food and camping supplies from the car into a sturdy fourteen-foot wooden boat, and then the children climbed in, too. As they set out across the lake, Maureen placed her hand next to her father's on the tiller, as if she, the boat's smallest passenger, were steering their ship. Slowly they headed toward the lake's northern peninsula, accessible only by water.

On the boat, they pushed through choppy waves and clouds of mosquitoes. They passed rock cliffs and dense woodland crowding the shore. The puttering cruise took thirty minutes until they pulled up to a small bay.

Their bay.

Her brothers jumped out, splashing through shallow water to shore. When she was really young, one of Maureen's parents would pluck her out of the boat and place her in the water, where she'd freeze, clutch onto the side of the boat, and refuse to take even one step, sure the knee-deep water would swallow her up. But as she grew older, she and her cousin leaped toward the land as avidly as her two brothers.

The Wiltons didn't own the whole peninsula, but it often felt like they did, as there was so rarely another human within sight. The bathroom was a wooden box built around a bucket, no walls, no shower, just trees for privacy as far as you could see. Their plot was so private that on one visit, after working on their land all day, her father decided to take off his filthy clothes and wash off in the lake. He was very proper, so he was not typically one to swim in the nude. After diving in, he resurfaced to find himself face-to-face with a fisherman.

Initially, their untamed land in that little bay held only the promise of something more. There was a pump and a picnic table, but beyond that, the only structures were natural. Rocks to scramble up, trees to climb and hide behind, and all sorts of birds and fish and other wildlife. Maureen's parents had hoped to build something eventually, but for many years their only shelter was a tent—a very cozy home for two adults and three or four children, depending on Tom's attendance. For Maureen, these were the best two weeks of the whole year, filled with endless swimming, running, playing, and exploring.

Maureen and Tom were close in age and inseparable during the summers at the lake. Once, when Margaret reported that a mother raccoon had visited their campsite during the night, the two children hatched a plan. If there was a mother raccoon around, they thought, she'd definitely want the company of some babies. They made a sign: BABY RACCOONS FOR SALE. And then they waited, only to be disappointed that not a single raccoon took them up on the offer.

***

And then, faster than ever seemed possible, the two weeks at the lake would end. The Wilton family rushed back on the boat, back in the car, and back to their suburban routine. Maureen never seemed to get enough time at her favorite place. The trip to Doe Lake was always a highlight.

But there were plenty of other bright spots. On a warm weekend once a year, Maclean Hunter would invite all its local employees and their families for food and activities at a grassy park on Musselman's Lake, just north of Toronto. Dozens of kids whirled and tussled and played in the open air. Maureen laughed watching Dan and Gord, swaddled up to their armpits, hop and fall over during the potato sack races. But Maureen's favorite event by far was the one she participated in: the cross-park dash.

Maureen was tiny for her age, but when you grow up with two older brothers, keeping up is a requirement. So when twenty-odd boys and girls of every age lined up at the park to race, Maureen claimed a spot and eyed the finish.

With her first big step, Maureen exhaled. Arms held away from her body and legs churning, she sped over the lawn, powered by pure excitement.

"Run!" her family cheered from the sideline.

Her body was working so hard that the only clear thought her brain could muster was *I love this*. It didn't matter whether she won or not (she didn't). The sprint just felt good.

But as more weekends went by, the memory of that rare fun faded. She played dolls and dress-up with neighborhood friends, did schoolwork, and rode bikes with her brothers.

Although she loved playing tag and running around the neighborhood, she didn't encounter many opportunities to race in any organized fashion. In gym class she'd race against classmates from time to time. And once, when she was seven, Maureen remembers being the only one punished for running down the halls of her grade school with a few other kids.

Maureen immediately fessed up to it.

"Well, what did you learn?" Margaret asked when her daughter returned home.

"Do not admit it," Maureen said, giving the reply she knew her mother wanted to hear.

It wouldn't be the last time Maureen would get in trouble for running or the last time Margaret defended it.

When Maureen was in grade three, her parents decided to move the family closer to Toronto. Her father was tired of the long commute, and her oldest brother, Gord, was entering high school. Margaret wanted him in Catholic school, and there wasn't a parochial high school in their small town. No one in the family wanted to move back to their old neighborhood, so they settled on North York, a blooming suburb east of downtown

Toronto. They moved into a three-bedroom semi-detached home in the leafy neighborhood.

***

One evening after school, Maureen sat at her family's metal kitchen table, pushing her food around her plate. Her brother Gord had just come home late from a track-and-field meet at his high school. He walked up to the table with a crisp blue ribbon from the 50-yard dash. The flash of color caught the interest of Maureen and her middle brother, Dan.

"How did you get that?" Maureen asked.

"Running in a race," said Gordon, pulling out a chair to sit down.

"A race?" Dan asked.

"Yeah, at school."

Maureen and Dan looked at each other.

"I want to win a ribbon," said Dan.

"Oh, it would be so wonderful to win a ribbon," Maureen said. "I want to run in a race."

3

It was an innocent request. If running a race was what it took to get a ribbon, then Maureen wanted to run a race. Simple, right? All her parents needed to do was find her a team and sign her up. Maureen would practice and maybe, just maybe, she'd work hard enough and become fast enough to finish in the top three. Then: bam! A ribbon.

But there was a catch—a big one.

In 1964, most girls just didn't run—not on teams or in organized races. People thought the idea was unladylike. Girls weren't supposed to sweat or exhaust themselves or breathe hard. Sure, girls could *try* to find a place to run. But they'd be judged.

Most grade schools and many high schools in Canada and the United States didn't offer cross-country or track programs for girls. Outside of school? Good luck finding a club. Boys, even the younger ones, could register with relative ease. But girls? They had to search hard, travel long distances, or find something else to do.

Which meant that even though Maureen wanted to

take up a new sport, finding a running team or club, even in a major metropolitan area of Canada, was difficult. Say she *could* find a group to run with—Maureen was younger than the sport's governing body allowed in competition.

Maureen didn't know any of this. In her house, she did what her brothers did. And her parents encouraged it. Like her brother Dan, she had two swift legs and a desire for a shiny blue prize. Her mom and dad weren't going to shut her down before at least looking into some options. They acted as a shield, keeping her dreams for a ribbon safe from the poisonous societal beliefs that had squelched the dreams of countless girls before Maureen.

Because Maureen was far from the first girl who wanted to run. She was not the only one who had yearned for a ribbon or gotten addicted to the joy of letting your legs rip down the road. For most girls before her, that dream had been stamped out. Some lacked parental support, others couldn't find a running club or competitions that would admit them. Many just gave up their running dreams and defaulted to a sport that was considered more feminine, like swimming.

But there was one moment, several decades before Maureen was born, when it seemed that things were about to change for female runners. And this moment came in the summer of 1928, when, for the first time ever, women were allowed to run in the Olympic Games.

***

"On your mark."

The women crouched down, fingers just behind the white chalk line, readying themselves to run before the world.

It was July 31, 1928. The weather in Amsterdam that day was humid and hot. Athletes complained that the cinder track felt soggy, more like a swamp than a speedway. But that wasn't the only problem. Just minutes before the pistol would fire to start the final of the 100-meter dash, sixteen-year-old Betty Robinson, an American, was in the locker room, worrying that she wouldn't make it to the start at all. After qualifying in her race the day before, she'd arrived on time for the final showdown. She tended to her feet by lancing blisters and rubbing toes (running shoes in those days were seriously uncomfortable). Then she reached inside her bag. Instead of finding a normal pair of track shoes, she'd pulled out two left-footed ones.

In an impromptu race-before-the-race, her coach sent someone sprinting to her room on the ship that housed the American team to get the right one—literally, the *right* one. When he returned, Betty knotted the laces and hustled out to the field, making it into the stadium just before the finals of the 100-meter race.

She crouched in a ball of tense muscles between two Canadians, Fanny Rosenfeld, who went by Bobbie, and Myrtle Cook.

Bobbie was tall and strong, built like a tree with short bobbed hair (hence the nickname). She was the kind of athlete who excelled at everything—tennis, hockey, basketball, and baseball. As the authors of a 1981 book about Canada's most famous female athletes noted, "The most efficient way to summarize Bobbie Rosenfeld's career in sport is to say that she was not good at swimming," because she was good at almost everything else.

Myrtle was shorter, with wild waves of dark bobbed hair. At twenty-six, she was older than many of the other competitors but had years of sports experience, including tennis, bowling, cycling, and canoeing.

When the official shouted "Set," Betty leaned forward.

But before the starting gun fired, Myrtle leaped—a false start. She was visibly shaken by the mistake.

No doubt she was feeling the pressure. What was at stake?

Oh, just the first gold for a woman in the 100 meters. Global recognition for Canada. And the pressure to perform in front of tens of thousands of people, a scale of spectators she'd never experienced before arriving in Amsterdam for the Olympics. Just that.

She placed her hands down behind the line and attempted, unsuccessfully, to steady her breathing.

"Set."

Myrtle twitched. Officials ejected her for her second false start. As her teammates escorted her off, she wept.

Twenty-one-year-old Leni Schmidt from Germany was next. She launched off the starting line too early. And then when the runners reset, she false-started again. Leni left the track yelling. At first there were six runners. Now only four.

"Set."

The gun fired. Then—confusion. The crowd couldn't tell who was in the lead.

Betty and Bobbie crossed the finish side by side, both throwing their arms up to celebrate. It was so close that the officials had to deliberate. Their decision? At 12.3 seconds, Bobbie came in second for Canada. At 12.2 seconds, American Betty Robinson earned the first gold medal for women in track and field.

***

You'd expect women's track and field to take off in North America after their success. With role models like Betty and Bobbie, girls now had runners to look up to. Those girls might want to run themselves. Maybe schools and sports clubs would invest in programs that would train the next generation of great women track heroes.

It didn't happen. Here's why.

That year, the International Olympic Committee allowed women to compete in one other solo running event besides the 100 meters: the 800 meters. The 100 is the classic sprint distance and one of track and field's most high-profile races. Taking place on the straightaway of a 400-meter track, it's so short that there's no time to strategize about holding back early in order to push ahead at a certain moment. In the 100 meters, it's an all-out effort from the start to the finish. Which means that every step and every arm pump must be undertaken with machinelike intensity. It is a tough distance to race, unforgiving of even the smallest mistake.

The 800, however, is a brutal race in a different way. At two laps around the track (about half a mile), it's not long enough for runners to settle in to a comfortable pace. But it's not short enough to allow an all-out, spill-your-guts sprint like the 100. You can try. You might even feel good for 500 meters, after taking the first turn of the second lap. But on the backstretch your body will eventually, inevitably, revolt. Legs will scream, air will disappear. Your only hope is to ignore your body, which is begging you to slow down, as long as you can. As former professional runner Phoebe Wright said, "There are two ways to think about the 800: Both are crazy. You can brainwash yourself into thinking you're not hurting, or you can . . . acknowledge you're hurting but tell yourself you like it." It's a race where you just try to stay alive.

Which didn't sit well for critics of women's distance running. They saw the 800 as a race that would do damage to the fragile female physique. If women *had* to run (insert disapproving glance), the twelve-second effort in the 100 was less likely to cause serious bodily harm. At eight times the distance, critics were certain the brutal 800 would destroy a woman.

The critics glared at the track during the 1928 Olympics, perhaps some of them hoping their macabre predictions would prove true.

The weather certainly gave critics a lot of help. It was the hottest day of the games. Rain in the morning boosted the humidity. In the steamy heat, racers pulled at their singlets, peeling the heavy fabric off sweaty torsos before the race even started. Reporters took bets on which runners would crumble.

Two Canadians and one American had advanced to the 800-meter final. Two other runners, Germany's Lina Radke-Batschauer and Sweden's Inga Gentzel, had both at one time held the world record in the event. Yes, the weather conditions were extreme. But the nine women had trained for this event, some for years. They were the best in the world. They knew what they were up against. When the pistol cracked, the women took off at a screaming pace. At the 400-meter mark—one lap—Inga held the lead. The rest followed in single file on the inside lane (the fastest part of the track, because it's the shortest distance around the oval). On the backstretch, just as the racers were trying to power through the wall of fatigue, Lina, the other world record holder in the event, pulled ahead. Kinue Hitomi of Japan matched Inga's effort, and the trio broke free, gaining several seconds on the rest of the field. When they finished, an official declared that Lina had won the gold for Germany, Kinue had won silver for Japan, and Inge had brought home bronze for Sweden. Incredibly, all three beat the previous world record time for the 800—and beat it despite the heat, the humidity, and the squishy track. The race was remarkable. And the incredible, taxing effort showed.

Two Canadians followed the medalists. One leaned into the finish and fell to the ground. She remained there for a few seconds, exhausted, before race officials pulled her up and assisted her away.

An experienced athlete knows that dealing with the discomfort during a race—and especially in the final push to the finish line—is part of the sport, as it is in any endurance sport. But for the critics? Every stumble, every grimace the women exhibited during and after the race became evidence. *That wasn't just a fall, it was a collapse. Those looks of agony weren't due to effort but from their fragile bodies breaking down.*

It wasn't difficult for reporters to play up the controversy.

One article said, "It was a pitiful spectacle: to see these girls tumble down after the finish like dead sparrows." There were reports of vomiting and crying, blood pouring out of wounded feet. They were called "wretched women." A reporter from the *Chicago Tribune* wrote, "Of the eight girls who finished, six of them fainted exhausted—a pitiful spectacle and a reproach to anyone who had anything to do with putting on a race of this kind." And in the *New York Times*: "The gals dropped in swooning heaps as if riddled by machine-gun fire." According to printed reports, it was a scene of carnage and weakness.

It didn't help that Betty Robinson, the sixteen-year-old winner of the 100-meter race, offered an unfortunate opinion. "The laws of nature never provided a girl with the physical equipment to withstand the grueling pace of such a grind," she said. Her fellow female runners were livid.

Never mind the weather, or that for any contestant regardless of gender the 800 is a spirit- and body-breaking endeavor. Never mind that at this same Olympics, Paavo Nurmi, considered one of the most successful male athletes in Olympic history, collapsed on the field after finishing second in his 5,000-meter race. When it looked like the women of the 800-meter final had barely survived, public opinion turned.

Critics of women's running claimed that women were too weak, that the sport would stop women from having children, that their uteruses would detatch—"wandering wombs," they called it—or that the women would grow facial hair or would become lesbians. Men decided that women belonged at home for their own safety, their own well-being, with their husbands, tending to the children.

A few voices of reason did speak up. The Canadian women's team manager marveled at the effort, especially the Canadians' push together at the end, saying it was "one of the finest exhibitions of sportsmanship ever witnessed on any track." One man judging the event wrote, "I was . . . on the spot at the time, I can therefore certify that there was nothing wrong with them, they burst into tears betraying their disappointment at having lost the race, a very feminine trait!" But these voices of reason were swallowed by outrage.

The International Olympic Committee, which had already made very clear that it was against women's participation, yanked the 800 from female competitions moving forward. In the 1932 and 1936 games—while men were able to compete at a range of distances, including the 100, 200, 400, 800, 1,500, 5,000, 10,000 meters, and the marathon—the longest race for women was the 100. After the disruption caused by World War II, the next Summer Olympics weren't held until 1948. At those games, the 200 was introduced for women. That was, they believed, the longest distance women should attempt.

This discrimination against women at the upper echelons of the sport had a chilling effect. Girls wouldn't have any female distance-running champions to admire. Schools didn't open up their track-and-field programs to girls. The Amateur Athletic Union barred women from participating in the longer road races that had begun cropping up for men. Women were told that if they wanted to run, they'd have to run short distances on courses without too much difficulty. It's hard to win a ribbon doing that.

***

Maureen was ten years old when her older brother Gord came home with a ribbon. As she gazed at the prize, she had no idea that the concerns of those in power in the 1920s were still the same concerns that justified keeping women from running farther than halfway around a track.

Luckily, no one in her family—not her mother, not her father, not her brothers—shared those same concerns. Nor did they believe, like so many others, that running just wasn't for girls. When Gord returned home one night with the news that he'd seen a coach training his daughter at a nearby high school track, Maureen's mother said, "Let's go."

The next day, they did.

4

The quarter-mile track next to Earl Haig Secondary
School was more rectangle than oval. It traced a cinder-
and-clay path around well-kept infield grass, in the
shadow of the three-story brick school.

As Margaret parked her car, Maureen and her
brother Dan watched as high school boys reached for
their toes, swung their legs, and puttered at a lazy jog,
getting ready for after-school track practice.

It was spring. The weather felt pleasant, not too hot
and not too cold. Maureen didn't know it yet, but this
was the ideal condition to run long, sustained miles.

The trio spotted the coach almost immediately. A
motionless totem in the midst of dozens of hyperener-
getic teens. Next to him stood a young girl.

Margaret turned to Maureen in the front seat and
Dan in the back. "You see him?" she said, pointing to the
field. "He's right there."

"What? You mean you're not going with us?" Maureen asked, shocked that her mom wanted them to
introduce themselves.

"Just go ask him if you can run."

Maureen and Dan exited the car furtively, shuffling toward the field. Margaret watched from the window.

Dan, the more outgoing one, approached first. Maureen stayed a few feet behind, painfully aware of how much she stood out in this crowd. She was much younger and significantly shorter than anyone else on the field.

"Can my sister and I run with you today?" Dan asked after introducing himself.

"Sure thing!" the man said. He looked at Maureen and smiled, waving over the only other girl. "This is my daughter Brenda. I know she'd like to have a girl to run with."

Brenda was a head taller than Maureen, and at eleven, a year older. She had long brown hair fastened in a ponytail with wispy bangs and a wide smile. Maureen, still shy, looked at her nervously. They took to each other immediately.

Brenda's father's name was Sy Mah (pronounced "Sigh Mahhh"). Born in Canada in 1926, he was the son of Chinese immigrants. He taught physical education at Earl Haig, and he coached the boys' track team. He was lithe, with close-cropped black hair and dark-rimmed glasses. He had sweatpants tucked into white tube socks and Adidas shoes. He looked like someone who knew what he was doing on a track.

Sy explained the day's workout. Everyone but Maureen and Dan would run twelve 220s. The newcomers would only run eight. One full lap on the Earl Haig track was equal to a quarter mile or 440 yards, so he wanted them to run fast for half a lap, then jog slowly back to the start to catch their breath before starting again. To Maureen, it sounded like math—which she liked—but this math didn't make much sense. Sy told Maureen and Dan they'd get the hang of it. The goal for today: watch, learn, and don't burn out.

Sy stood on the grass just beyond a concrete curb that separated the track from the infield. He had all the kids line up next to him. Dan blended right in with the boys. Maureen tucked in next to Brenda.

"On your mark," said Sy, looking at his stopwatch. "Get set..."

Maureen inhaled her last easy breath.

"Go."

Maureen's legs had only one setting: fast. She ran like she'd been conditioned to run outside. She ran like Gord was on her heels about to tag her out. She ran as if she had the perfect hide-and-seek spot but it was a nine-second sprint away and Dan was counting to ten. She ran like she was competing against a park full of children at her father's company picnic or like she was chasing her cousin at the lake. The feeling of her feet crunching against the cinder track and her arms rippling through the air felt like it did all those times she'd run before. It felt good. And right. And like she could do it forever.

But even over half a lap, she kept fading behind Brenda. They'd start together, but Brenda floated away. She became a churn of legs and shrinking ponytail. Brenda wasn't just running with the high school boys, she was running ahead of them. Watching Brenda tear around the track exhilarated Maureen. The other girl's effort compelled Maureen to push even harder.

When Maureen reached the finishing mark on the other side of the track, an assistant coach, whom everyone called Mr. A., read out times from his stopwatch as the runners passed. Then they'd walk or jog back to Sy and start another 220 interval together.

At every finish, Brenda waited for the two newcomers. Maureen had a distinct feeling that following in Brenda's literal footsteps would guide her to a crisp blue ribbon. She wanted one as quickly as possible. Maybe a few more of these 220s and she'd get there.

"That's enough," Sy barked. Maureen and Dan had finished eight sprints. Sy told them their practice was over.

"Really?" Maureen half asked, half begged, glancing at Sy and then her mom, who had left the car and perched at the side of the track. "Do we have to quit?"

Dan shot her a look. "Keep quiet," he said. It was clear he did not share her zeal for the lung- and leg-busting workout.

Maureen ignored her brother. "Do we have to stop?"

"Come back tomorrow," said Sy with an amused smile. "We'll do it again."

***

This one-hour practice? With this man and his daughter on this track out of all the tracks in North America? It changed everything for Maureen. Dan, not so much. He dropped out not long after he started.

From now on, Monday through Thursday, Maureen went to school, came home to complete homework, and ate an early dinner before riding her bike to Earl Haig to run with Brenda at the track.

Maureen learned about those numbers—440s, 220s, and 110s. These numbers meant the number of yards she was expected to run at one time and were roughly equivalent to 400s, 200s, and 100s on a track that went by metric measurements. A 440 lap was also known as a quarter, short for a quarter of a mile. And 110s were run in the track's grassy middle, from goalpost to goalpost. Those 110s in particular were run *as fast as humanly possible*, and they hurt.

In each of these practices, Maureen followed Brenda's ponytail diligently, dreaming about the day she could keep up. The two young runners quickly became friends. Before Maureen showed up, Brenda had been an outsider at her father's practices with the high school team. And in Brenda, Maureen found someone to look up to, someone to run with, and someone to talk about running with. Because once Maureen started in the sport, her passion for it consumed everything. School friendships faded. She organized her life to accommodate it.

She now did her homework in bursts, like 110 repeats. She sat down and raced through her assignments at the dining room table as soon as she got home from school and then again after practice.

She started drinking Ovaltine. Its vitamin-rich, vaguely chocolate flavor was supposed to help her performance, so she choked it down. And she kept a box of raisins in her pocket for a little energy injection during the day. In fact, she was so frequently found with raisins that kids at school began calling her "Raisin Girl," a name that Maureen never liked. The other kids didn't understand that the small box wasn't a weird snack. It was rocket fuel. Not that they would ever know. Maureen didn't talk to anyone at school about her running. She didn't want to have to deal with their confused questions. *A girl? Running? Why?* Better to keep the running to herself . . . at least for the time being. Because what she had at the track with Brenda? It was pure joy.

5

"I want to go! Why can't I go?"

Sy looked at Maureen. "You haven't been training that long."

Maureen was obsessed with running, but begging wouldn't get her into the meet. What she needed was practice.

"I can go!" she proclaimed defiantly.

"Not this time."

Maureen was crushed. She wanted to test her legs. She wanted to know what would happen if she dialed them up to full power. Would she be able to keep up? To get a ribbon, you have to race, but Sy wasn't allowing it.

One small solace: Brenda was on her side—and not just because it was nice having another girl on the team, but because Brenda knew what it felt like to be told that you weren't allowed to participate in a race.

***

Brenda had started running with her father because there was a time, when she was very young, when it looked like she wouldn't be able to do much physical activity at all. She'd had pneumonia repeatedly, and the doctor feared her sickly condition might last all her life. But when Brenda began swimming regularly, her father saw her condition improve. He wondered if more exercise might help. As a coach and physical education teacher, Sy used his skills to train her. He taught Brenda how to run, to extraordinary results. Brenda not only felt better, but her legs and lungs grew stronger. On the track, she could fly.

With Brenda as its first member, Sy founded the North York Track Club. He began entering his daughter in track meets around the region. Brenda was a spectacle. Young, fast, and female. Reporters flocked. With the warmth and confidence of a practiced showman, Sy shared her training regimen with local press. He publicly expressed skepticism about the common ideas and established rules surrounding young girls and running. He didn't believe, for instance, that girls should be limited to short distances. Sprinting was likely harder on their bodies than running long distances. And age limitations? They were nonsense.

The Canadian Amateur Athletic Union, the organization that outlines the general rules and regulations for non-elite sporting events for people of every age, did not agree. Gender rules, age limitations, and distance caps were all rules instated and enforced by the Canadian AAU.

On the track, Sy believed Brenda was a compelling argument against the establishment. He signed her up for races that would test the boundaries of what the rules would allow. These races raised her profile, and importantly, his, too.

In March 1964, Sy entered Brenda into the girls' Canadian Championships in Hamilton, Ontario.

The race was about an hour's drive away. There were lots of events that day, but Brenda planned to run the 880, the imperial equivalent to the metric 800, the notoriously hard race that had caused such an uproar at the Olympics four decades earlier. Whether calculated in yards or meters, however, the distance didn't faze her. She'd been training—meticulously, religiously—for it.

When it was time for the event, an official called the girls to the track. Seventeen gathered around as he delivered the day's instructions.

Among the competitors was seventeen-year-old Abby Hoffman, who in just a few months would fly to Tokyo to represent Canada in the Olympics. Abby was tall, around five feet, nine inches, with long muscular limbs and short curly hair. As a young girl, Abby had played competitive hockey on an all-boys team. Or at least the organization thought it was an all-boys team. Little did they know that the team's short-haired goalie "Ab" was actually a girl. Assuming she was a boy (and that Abby was following the rules that barred girls from participating), the registering official took only a passing glance at her birth certificate, admitting her without noticing the name "Abigail" or that her gender was indicated as "female." Officials eventually realized they'd made a mistake and kicked her off the team for the next season, but that setback didn't stall her athletic career. As a teen, Abby became one of Canada's best runners in the 880 (half mile) and 440 (quarter mile).

Brenda, all seventy-three pounds and four feet, eight inches of her (a full foot shorter than the future Olympian), looked like a wispy child comparatively.

Ralph Adams, the race director, cut through the lanes of the track and into the middle green. He wore a suit and bow tie. Pinned to a lapel, a ribbon pronounced his authority. OFFICIAL, it read.

When he reached the girls, he grabbed Brenda by the arm.

There was a gasp from the stands. The race director was several times Brenda's size. He smiled as he gripped her arm, escorting her away from the group.

Brenda burst into tears in what must have been a mix of surprise, humiliation, and disappointment.

The crowd began to boo and jeer. Once he reached her father, Adams explained that at eleven years old, Brenda was too young to run. Sy responded as calmly as he could: Brenda had been cleared by a doctor to run; she had lots of experience with 880s; she regularly covered a mile and a half or more during practice.

The spectators hissed and yelled—a persuasive cacophony of displeasure, all directed at the man in the blazer.

The race director gave in. As he turned around and walked Brenda back toward the starting line—never once letting go of her arm—the crowd burst into cheers and applause. Brenda, who was finally released from his claws and the public mortification, wiped her tears away. The girls—eleven-year-old Brenda included—tensed at the line.

The starter's pistol sounded.

From the start, Brenda was rattled. The track was small, and reaching the 880 finish meant running six tight laps. She had a hard time finding her rhythm, her strength. Abby burst to the front. Brenda didn't even try to keep up. Before the final lap, she lagged to tenth place. But to the crowd, she was clearly the favorite. Spectators roared during Brenda's last loop, giving her a final boost. She weaved through the giants in front of her, passing one, two, then three girls before crossing the finish.

In the *Toronto Globe and Mail* that Monday, Brenda is pictured twice. Once being escorted off the field, wiping her tears with the palm of her hand, and a second time, smiling next to the event's president, who'd given her a small trophy for her effort. She told the reporter, "I was really disappointed when he came over to me. I guess it did upset me and I might have run faster."

It would probably have helped if she'd had a friend beside her that day. Which is why she lobbied her father to let Maureen race.

Maureen didn't know why Sy wouldn't let her go, but maybe it had something to do with how Brenda had been treated. If he was going to send someone even younger, smaller, and less experienced, he wanted to know—and to show everyone else watching and reading the newspaper reports—that he had her training under control. She had to be ready.

In some ways, the girls' potential for long-term success was tied to their short-term performance. If they collapsed on the track, it would be harder to make the case that they should run again. So Sy stressed practice,

practice, practice, until finally he determined Maureen had the experience to compete.

***

At her first race, Maureen was buoyant. She followed Brenda's lead. They did jumping jacks, completed a short warm-up jog around the field, and threw in a few sprints back and forth. Loose groups of boys and girls in uniforms gathered in the bleachers and beside the track preparing for the day's events.

Maureen was giddy. She was the second member of Sy's North York Track Club—and proud to wear the club's jersey. That yellow tank top with a diagonal red stripe from right shoulder to left hip with the words NORTH YORK sliding along it? That was her ticket. Maureen was finally allowed to compete for a ribbon.

The meet at Northview Heights Collegiate Institute was designed for boys and girls her age, which meant there was no threat of ejection. Maureen had prepared to run the 440-yard race, ready for an all-out sprint once around the track.

The Saturday spring weather was unseasonably warm. It may have been uncomfortable for some of the runners, but not Maureen. The heat slid off her like the complaints of her competitors. It didn't bother her, the sunshine. She hadn't even broken a sweat.

Fewer than ten girls lined up at the white line of Maureen's race. Her parents watched from the bleachers, and Sy and Brenda watched from the sidelines, each one sending silent encouragement. Maureen's feet dug into the loose cinder-and-clay surface of the track. Her body was wound tight, like a rock about to launch out of a slingshot.

Maureen leaned forward, her front leg increasing its bend slightly.

For the ribbon, Maureen thought as the starter's pistol fired.

She bounded forward, using every muscle, extending every breath. She felt free. Sure, her lungs strained and tingled, but pent-up energy from weeks of anticipation flooded her system.

Until it didn't. Excitement turned to pain. Adrenaline to lactic acid. She'd made it 220 yards and felt like she had nothing left.

At first the experience was disorienting, like reaching for a glass of water on your nightstand that's no longer there. *Why am I slowing down?* Then it was demoralizing.

Two runners passed her right at the end, carrying with them Maureen's hope for a ribbon.

When she finally reached the finish, she certainly wasn't last, but she was also far from where she would have been had her burst from the start lasted longer. She was upset by her performance and disappointed that she wouldn't get a ribbon.

"Way to go!" said Maureen's dad.

Maureen's breathing may have returned to normal, but her mood was low.

Did you not see that? thought Maureen. *Were you not watching all those people passing me? That's not what I had in mind.*

"Thanks," she said out loud, sounding more like a deflated balloon than a grateful daughter. "It wasn't that great."

"Oh no, you did fine. You did good," Roger said.

"Next time," said Sy gently, "go out a little bit slower and save some for the end."

Even with the words of encouragement, Maureen held on to her devastation. She took it home and slept with the feeling.

On Sunday morning, she woke up and ran. She immediately felt better.

6

By the fall of 1964, Maureen had spent six months as a member of the North York Track Club. She'd run through the summer—the season in Ontario when the heat is thick and heavy. When the first cool days arrived, Maureen's routine didn't fluctuate. She'd already spent week after week running in lung-searing, leg-aching intervals, grinding away on the dusty surface of the track at Earl Haig Secondary School, named after a senior British commander from the First World War.

Under Sy's direction, Maureen's training had escalated quickly. She and Brenda now logged nearly seven miles a day, six days a week. But these miles weren't always the slow and continuous kind. Repeats of 440s, 220s, or 110s chopped up the workout in short bursts of breath-stealing speed. Maureen acclimated to the persistent, satisfying shadow of discomfort. She learned not to panic. She learned that the harder she worked, the better she felt.

She now understood how to avoid the embarrassment of her first race. Sy taught Brenda and Maureen that finishing strong meant understanding pace—the optimal speed that you run to cover a certain distance. For a short sprint, you dial up your speed to blazing fast; it's what you can maintain if you're running for only a few seconds. In a several-mile run, you turn your speed way down to the fastest tempo you can maintain over the whole distance, hopefully allowing for a little extra burst of effort at the end. The challenge is a bit like choosing a novel for a road trip. Ideally, you want a book that finishes right as you reach your destination, not an hour before, not an hour after.

Beginners learn pace with a stopwatch. It helps to have a coach barking out the time as they finish each loop so they can make adjustments to their speed while they circle around the track without having to consult a watch on the go. With practice and experience, Maureen became adept at intuiting her pace without a watch. From her heart rate, breathing, and leg turnover, she learned how to *feel* the difference between a sixty eight-second 440 versus a seventy-second one.

But as she learned more and ran stronger, she realized her initial desire to win a ribbon was too modest a goal. In fact, with so few girls her age who ran, it was surprisingly easy to get one. So easy that the first one she earned—as a middle-of-the-pack finisher in a race—didn't feel that remarkable. That's because ribbons were given to everyone *except* the winner.

Maureen no longer wanted just a ribbon. She wanted what Brenda earned race after race: a little pedestal with a gold runner on top. Maureen wanted a winner's trophy. To get one, though, she'd have to defeat her swifter friend. She'd have to take down the mighty Brenda Mah.

***

Pass them like you mean it. Pass them like you mean it. On the track, Maureen learned to pass people with confidence and decisiveness. She didn't want to give them a moment to think, *Can I pick up my pace and stop this competitor from passing me? Can I catch her?*

This must have been shocking for the older runners to experience, to have this little twig of a girl whip by and leave them in the dust.

But Maureen also knew what it felt like to be passed with authority. When Brenda performed the same trick, Maureen could never catch her. She lost to Brenda yet again at a subsequent meet at Northview Collegiate in the fall of 1964.

After the award ceremony, Brenda walked over, trophy in hand. "Good job," Brenda said, giving Maureen's elbow a nudge with her own. Maureen had finished in the top three and received a plaque, but Brenda knew Maureen wanted first.

"I'm never going to beat you!" complained Maureen. No matter how much she'd improved, how confidently she passed the other runners, how powerful her stride, it wasn't enough.

"You'll beat me," said Brenda.

"I haven't yet!"

"You will," said Brenda. And then Brenda presented Maureen with a modest golden base with a runner on top. It was the winner's trophy. "Here, you have mine."

Maureen gasped, her face blooming with a look of disbelief.

"Your first trophy," said Brenda. "You deserve it."

"But—"

"The first, but not the last, I promise."

Maureen was touched by her friend's generosity and would soon learn just how right Brenda's prediction was.

***

Newspaper reporters have an old aphorism: "Dog Bites Man" isn't news. But "Man Bites Dog"? That's worth putting in the paper. In the fall of 1964, "Boys Run Track" wasn't really news—maybe a few lines on page two of the sports section. But "Girls Run Track"? The reporters flocked to get the scoop on that story.

Articles ran in the Toronto papers recounting the

girls' efforts with flair. In one article, Maureen was the "Mighty Missile" and Brenda the "Pigtail Wonder." Neither name stuck, but it gave their repeated first- and second-place or even sixth-place finishes an allure— almost like Maureen and Brenda flew to the finish as kid superheroes.

They were a good story. On more than one occasion, Sy invited a newspaper reporter and photographer to visit Earl Haig to get a better look at the girls' training. And what they found was . . . *unconventional.*

Sy wanted the girls to get not only faster, but stronger. So during the occasional practice, he made them climb stairs. His take on the stair climb didn't involve leaping up stadium steps two at a time. First, because there were no stadium steps at the track. Second, speed wasn't the goal, strength was. Which meant they needed to add weight. That weight came from carrying other people piggyback.

During one journalist's visit, Brenda hauled her father up the stairs wearing her North York jersey and shorts. She smiled as she took each step. Even with Sy on her back, Brenda looked energetic and strong.

Sy was slim and not particularly tall, but even so, he towered over his daughter. His hands were giant on her shoulders. He leaned back and laughed, almost as if he knew how curious it would look to the photographer taking their picture.

The North York Track Club was quite the spectacle. On another occasion, a photographer captured Maureen and Brenda leading a pack of high school boys around the Earl Haig track. All around, the trees had shed their leaves. Where the boys ran in shorts and hooded sweatshirts, their faces betraying some amusement, Maureen and Brenda led the pack wearing their sleeveless North York jerseys and shorts, keeping their eyes focused on the empty lanes ahead.

It must have been a bit shocking for the men and women of Toronto, Ontario, when they opened their morning paper with a cup of coffee in hand and saw a four-foot-four-inch, fifty-six-pound, ten-year-old girl out ahead of teenage boy runners.

Sy knew how this would look. He orchestrated opportunities to show off the girls and get their names in the papers. On their way home from races, he made sure to stop at a pay phone to deliver his team's results to various sports reporters.

On Halloween, Sy finagled his biggest spectacle yet: two Saturday races in two different provinces scheduled just two hours apart. Event one would take place in Montreal, Quebec. Event two would take place in

Ottawa, Ontario, Canada's capital city. The catch: Even speeding along the Trans-Canada Highway, there wasn't enough time to cover the 125-mile distance and get to the second race on time. Sy had to get creative.

For the scheme to work, Maureen's father, Roger, played a key role. First, he drove Brenda, Maureen, and Sy to Montreal, a five-and-a-half-hour trip. The foursome arrived late Friday evening. As the girls got settled in the hotel room, Roger jumped back into the car. He needed to practice. The girls would need to hop on an airplane to arrive at the second meet on time—and because of the expense, neither Roger or Sy could fly with them. There was only a tiny window between the end of the first meet at the McGill University stadium and the departure of the flight at the Montreal airport. So Roger practiced the trip from McGill to the airport, driving back and forth in the dead of night, making sure he knew the route by heart, looking for shortcuts in case of traffic.

When Brenda and Maureen got up the next morning, the clock started ticking. If they were going to pull off this stunt, everything had to go right. Maureen was unfazed by this pressure. Her father, on the other hand, was a bundle of nerves.

Roger drove Maureen, Brenda, and Sy to the McGill stadium in downtown Montreal late in the morning. They were right on time.

The university stadium was monstrous compared to the Earl Haig track. Towering bleachers ascended at steep angles toward the sky, framing stately tall buildings made of gray stone next to the green peak of Mount Royal.

The Quebec AAU cross-country championship was a difficult challenge for the two young girls.

Sy had told them that this was not their race. He told them to reserve their energy for Ottawa. But when the starting gun cracked for the three-quarter-mile race, Maureen's and Brenda's easy pace kept them in the top three. The other runners fell farther and farther behind. For a "short distance" race that Sy did not expect them to win, Brenda finished in three minutes and forty-two seconds to claim an impressive second, and Maureen finished third.

Roger was standing by, ready to whisk the girls and their coach away. They had another race to win—a race to the airport. Just as Roger had anticipated, the traffic downtown was thick. Thanks to his training the night before, he weaved through it with confidence.

Roger pulled up to Dorval Airport just a few minutes before the flight to Ottawa was scheduled to leave. Airport security was lax to nonexistent in the 1960s, so Brenda and Maureen were able to run right onto the tarmac with their gym bags. The stewardess waited at the door while the girls speedily climbed up the stairs to the plane. At the top, Maureen froze. She'd never been on a plane before. She'd been so focused on making it to this spot on time that she didn't have a moment to think about what this meant. Flying. In the air. Without any parents.

The stewardess gave Maureen a friendly nudge and told her to get to her seat quickly. Maureen did what she was told. Now the race to the next event was in others' hands. Thankfully, the flight was quick. When they landed, ten-year-old Maureen and eleven-year-old Brenda hopped in a taxi that drove them to the Provincial cross-country championships in Ottawa. The girls arrived just before the two P.M. start of their second race. Sy's plan had worked!

This event doubled the distance of that morning's race, which was good since both Maureen and Brenda preferred the longer distance.

Their instructions from Sy were to keep pace with the lead runners at first, not to go all out, so they could get to know the course. The girls followed his directions. When the gun went off for the second time that day, they held back, sticking with the pack . . . for a time. But the pace set by the other runners started to feel uncomfortably slow. They'd been pent up in a car and an airplane for the last two hours; their legs wanted to *go*.

With Sy and Roger still driving from Montreal, Brenda decided to overrule her dad's advice. She increased her speed and took an early lead. Once she took it, she didn't let go. Brenda finished in first place in ten minutes and one second. The next-best finisher was almost a whole minute behind her. Maureen came in third.

At the conclusion of this *Amazing Race*–type scramble, Maureen and Brenda faced a crowd of reporters. They smiled, holding up their medals for the photographers. The girls were pleased with their performance. Sy's stunt got lots of coverage in the papers. The two families were thrilled with how the whole thing fell into place.

But not everyone else was.

7

Maureen's mom, Margaret, meticulously cut out every newspaper article with Maureen's name in it. In red pencil or blue pen, she drew a neat square around the passages where her daughter's achievements were mentioned, and then she taped the articles into a scrapbook. One day in the future, Maureen might appreciate these records of her early—and already trailblazing—running career. But with more and more clippings, more and more attention, these articles also became a time capsule of official objections.

"I don't think it's healthy for children to be entered in highly competitive races. They haven't reached the age where they're past playing children's games. I think they should compete against girls in their own age class," said Margaret Lord, president of the Southwestern Ontario branch of the AAU in an article from November 1964.

Other adults—even ones with official running titles—said the girls were too young, too frail. They questioned their training and readiness.

By taping these articles in the scrapbook, too, Margaret didn't shield her daughter from the objections, but she also didn't pay them much attention. Her daughter was working hard—a quality that was very important to Margaret. Maureen's passion for running was doing her some good. Margaret saw it, and everyone else who knew Maureen did, too. When she and Roger got an opportunity to speak to a reporter about Maureen's running, they offered their full support.

Roger told the reporter that running helped Maureen learn to budget her time. Her schoolwork was improving, and she'd lost interest in television. She "hasn't missed a day of school in two years," added Margaret.

"She used to eat like a bird," Roger said. "Now she's got a fine appetite."

Whenever Margaret sat on the sidelines during a practice at Earl Haig, she saw her daughter positively giddy. During workouts Maureen and Brenda joked and laughed as much as they could in spite of being completely out of breath.

And so, Margaret kept snipping off bits of the thin broadsheets and gluing them into the books. Good, historic, bad, and everything in between—she wanted to preserve this chapter of Maureen's life.

***

The day before Maureen turned eleven, she woke up across the border in New York State in the house of Anne Cirulnick. Anne was the race director of the Eastern United States AAU cross-country championships and a longtime runner herself. She'd watched the North York girls' accomplishments in the papers and reached out to Sy to invite them to what would be one of the largest cross-country women's races ever held in the United States: thirty-seven women, up from about fifteen the year before.

If they were able to come, she said, Sy and the girls were welcome to stay at her house—which is how Maureen came to wake up on Long Island this particular Sunday, the day before her birthday.

On Saturday, they'd spent more than eight hours in Sy's station wagon, driving past Niagara Falls, straight south on the New York State Thruway to New York City, and then on to suburban Long Island.

Anne seemed genuinely thrilled to have the girls and their coach as her houseguests. First of all, she had made an exception for them. The Amateur Athletic Union had rules that banned girls younger than fourteen from competing in their races. But Anne was a physical therapist, and she called bunk.

Anne believed not only that the girls were capable of running against the eighteen-year-old Middle Atlantic champion Louise Hay and former U.S. National AAU 880 champion Grace Butcher (who was old enough to have a son older than Brenda), but that Maureen and Brenda would improve the competition.

"I knew from the records of these little girls that they were capable of handling this race. But I had no idea that they would be so good," Anne told a reporter after Brenda's third- and Maureen's sixth-place finish. (The top seven finishers got trophies. Maureen was determined to be one of them.) "We believe that we must encourage girls who show ability—that is why we waived the rules for Brenda and Maureen. We also dread to think what these girls will do to our American girls next year, but they will be most welcome to come back again."

Brenda was thankful for the warm reception, since her memory of being banned from running due to her age was still fresh. "I wish we could move to New York where we would have more chances to run and be welcome at the meets," she said wistfully. But it was time to go.

The girls piled back into Sy's station wagon for the long drive home. On the way, they stopped for Chinese food. He introduced Maureen to wonton soup, which she instantly loved. But the stop was quick; they all had school the next day.

Maureen curled up on the floor of the backseat of the car. With the road rumbling underneath her and room to stretch out, it was by far the most comfortable place to lie down. She thought about the race she'd just finished and all the races ahead of her. Maureen fell asleep hugging her trophy. The first one she'd earned.

***

The next week, Margaret diligently cut out the articles detailing her daughter's race on Long Island.

She wasn't the only one who noticed Maureen's name in the paper. The press coverage had an unintended yet remarkable secondary effect. It served as an invitation, delivered into homes all over the Greater Toronto area. *You, too, could do what Maureen and Brenda are doing. You, too, can join the North York Track Club.* In the span of a year, Sy's club expanded from a team of two to a team of four and continued to increase from there.

Escaping their bedroom walls or front yard fences in the quiet town of North York, girls with dreams of running started showing up to the Earl Haig cinder track as if they were making a pilgrimage. Marg Robinson,

Nancy Bailey, and Eva Van Wouw started running with the team. Debbie Worrall joined. They came from different backgrounds. Their parents had different jobs. But they all had something in common. In a world telling them they shouldn't, they all wanted to run *fast*. And when a place popped up to let them do it, word spread quickly.

When a spunky, athletic-looking twelve-year-old named Jo-Ann Rowe came to the track with her father that summer, Sy wasted no time.

"Well, just start running," he said, pointing to the rectangular track.

Jo-Ann, like Maureen, was petite. Although technically Jo-Ann had a year and a few inches on her, next to everyone else, they were the small ones. Both had short bangs that stopped well before their eyebrows. Jo-Ann wore an ear-length bob, the same length as Maureen's hair before she'd started growing it out. Where Maureen was pure enthusiasm and excitement, Jo-Ann had power and confidence. Even at twelve, she showed up like a seasoned competitor.

Because she was. Jo-Ann had played basketball in a city league. She also played hockey and competed in waterskiing and downhill snow skiing events. She was not just active, but naturally athletic—the kind of kid who may have been the smallest on the basketball team but still played forward because she could out-jump and out-rebound the other players. Pick your sport: Jo-Ann was a force.

In a time when most of what women were doing in track and field qualified as a "first," Jo-Ann had a family history of female athletic prowess. Jo-Ann grew up listening to stories from her aunt, who was a basketball player and a sprinter. If there were few girls running in the 1960s, there were far fewer in the 1930s, and yet Margaret LaChapelle ran. She competed in the 1932 Olympic Trials for the 100-yard race, and she was on one of Canada's strongest women's relay teams. With this family history, Jo-Ann dreamed of finding athletic success on an international stage. That drive started from day one.

On her first day of practice, Jo-Ann glided around the track, completing lap after lap while her father chatted with Sy about the club.

"You better stop her," Jo-Ann's father said to Sy. "She'll run forever."

A girl named Joan Preston joined. She was a power-house who would expend every single thing she had on the course, often collapsing at the finish.

Sy recruited Sheila Meharg out of elementary school. She was a natural talent, with an easy laugh and an overall effervescence about her—a nice person to have around when the competition was tough, the workouts were brutal, and your legs were already tired.

And then there was Carol Haddrall.

Roughly ten miles north of North York, in a crowded low-income housing development, the sixteen-year-old girl dreamed of training to compete in the high jump.

Carol lived with her four sisters and their mom—a single parent putting in long hours to keep food on the table while making rent every month. They didn't own a car. Carol often longed to leave the cluster of brick buildings. So when she heard about a track club for girls, she leaped at the chance to join. It didn't matter if the track where they practiced was miles away and she couldn't afford the bus fare. She'd get there somehow.

"I heard there's a track club here," she said to Sy. "Can I high-jump?"

Sy looked at Carol and smiled. "Sure, but you have to do the warm-up first."

Little did Carol know, the warm-up was a lot of running. After five-plus miles, her body was worn out. She didn't have the energy to leap over a bar. Sy also didn't tell her that he'd moved away from training the girls in events like triple jump, high jump, and discus. Even when Maureen had started, they practiced these events only occasionally.

By the time Carol joined the club, Sy was singularly focused on finding opportunities for the girls to run long distances. Long-distance running was not what Carol had signed up for, but in practice, she followed the workouts that Sy prescribed. To her great surprise, Carol could manage the distances. And not just manage them—keep up.

That didn't mean things were easy. She told hardly anyone on the team where she lived. Sometimes, a friendly teacher who knew her circumstances would give her rides to practice. But often, Carol schlepped miles to Earl Haig on foot, only to endure Sy's brutal training regimen.

"I'm not getting up," Carol protested from the ground at a practice a few months after joining. After the last lap she'd collapsed to the grass as she struggled to catch her breath.

"Ten, nine, eight, seven..." Sy looked at his stopwatch from the grass infield just beside the track. He counted the seconds left until the girls needed to begin their fifteenth 440-yard interval.

The fabric of Carol's cotton blouse didn't breathe that well. Her worn sneakers were hand-me-downs. It was an unconventional outfit, not enhanced for performance in any way. It was the kind of running outfit you wore when your mom couldn't afford running clothes.

"Five, four, three . . ."

Lucky for Carol, the clothes don't make the runner.

By the time Sy got to "one," she'd peeled herself off the ground and jolted back into action, chasing after the rest of the runners.

8

"You hear about troubles with the younger generation," said Richmond Hill mayor Thomas Broadhurst as he passed out trophies. "But after what we've seen today, I don't think we have to worry."

Maureen had just wrapped up a day of running at the First Annual Richmond Hill Rose Bowl Road Races, where she had "thrilled the crowd" with a fourth-place finish in the three-quarter-mile event. Not first. Not second. Fourth. According to one published account, she "had the small crowd gaping and gasping as she churned down the homestretch, just barely visible among her larger opponents." The sight of her—a blur of birdlike arms and legs—among runners much older, taller, and stronger inspired delight. She reliably charmed crowds and mayors alike.

The girls' efforts were inspiring, but they were also record-breaking.

At a race series in Kitchener, Brenda's winning time for a two-and-a-quarter-mile race was nearly four minutes faster than the fastest boy in her age group. At the

Niagara District AAU championships in Buffalo, New York, Brenda slashed more than two minutes from the previous one-and-a-quarter-mile meet record, finishing in just under seven minutes. Oh, and that's after she'd run a race in Toronto the day before.

On the average race weekend, the North York girls took home two or three trophies each.

Part of their extraordinary acceleration as a team was Sy Mah's total dedication to the sport. Sy was a runner. He'd picked up running at age thirty-seven, not even a year before Maureen joined the club. And he was what could easily be described as obsessed. In addition to coaching the high school boys and the North York Track Club, Sy did his homework. He researched all the latest coaching techniques and kept up-to-date on the available physical-education and running-related research. He saw how hard the girls in the club pushed themselves, and so he pushed them a little harder. He'd assign workouts featuring 24 x 220, 20 x 440, 3 x 2-mile, or 5 x 1-mile intervals, and the girls learned that the faster they ran, the longer their recovery breaks between repeats. They used those slices of time for joking and talking—catching up with one another as they got their wind back. Their friendships motivated them just as much as the competition did.

Week after week Sy witnessed proof of their skills. And he was learning how best to show them off.

That meant untethering the workouts from the Earl Haig track. It meant running on roads. It meant going out in public. That meant leaving their sanctuary, their safe little quarter-mile bubble.

The girls needed to run longer, hillier distances if they were going to have success in cross-country races. On any given day, he might plan a route east through nearby neighborhoods, York Cemetery, and up to a park in an area known for its ostentatious mansions.

The girls had little time to daydream about the houses, though. They feared the hills. Sy loved giving hill repeats on Burnett Park's steep inclines, which challenged both legs and lungs. He wanted to give the girls the advantage on hilly cross-country courses. When other girls would slow down as their calves burned and their lungs strained, he'd teach his girls to accelerate.

Maureen loved the kind of pain the Burnett hills provided. And she savored the nature and scenery they'd get when they'd leave the track.

What she didn't love? Bystanders.

Where's the fire? someone might yell from his front porch.

They got comments about their baggy sweatpants a lot.

The girls dealt with these hecklers in different ways. When Jo-Ann rode her bike to practice, she hid her running shoes in her bike basket, to not draw attention. As she jogged on the street, Carol ducked behind a tree anytime she spotted someone she knew.

No matter how many records the team broke, how many races the team won, one offhand remark could spoil the moment. The comments happened regularly enough that when Maureen ran through neighborhoods with her teammates or on her own, she often felt apprehensive. It was only running through the cemetery that put her at ease. *The dead can't make fun of your clothes.*

At school, Maureen never talked about her trophies or her exploits. Her name was in the local sports section of the paper most weekends, so kids at school knew she ran. But she didn't volunteer the details of her trips to races outside the city and she rarely if ever spoke about the track practices that she went to each evening. When she had to run at school, she never ran all out. She didn't want to stand out, answer questions, or deal with comments. And Maureen hated bragging. She didn't want anyone thinking she was showing off.

Unless, of course, she was in the middle of an official race with her team, in which case, she counted on her performances to stand out for themselves.

Sometimes, though, that wasn't enough.

***

The morning in Baltimore was muggy and warm. By the first race of the day, the temperature had climbed to eighty-four degrees. Fifty-five women, ages ranging from twelve to thirty, lined up to run the mile-and-a-half cross-country course. Not a bad turnout for Catonsville Community College, a school just nine years old, established on a former dairy farm and featuring a library converted from a barn. The year prior, the community college put on the city's first-ever cross-country event. And today, even the mayor, Theodore McKeldin, showed up to ring in the second annual gathering.

Marie Mulder, a runner from Washington, DC, who was on the US national team, was expected to win. But Maureen was feeling strong at the start. The heat never bothered her; she didn't expect it to have any effect on her performance. Brenda and Jo-Ann, on the other hand, were both ill. Jo-Ann was getting over strep throat. The race director told the girls to take it easy.

"Never say die" was Sy's motto. He lobbed the phrase so often at the girls as they groaned about sore muscles, fatigue, cramps, or illness that the team internalized it, made it their mantra. Both Brenda and Jo-Ann determined to fight through the sick.

Ready.

Set.

The crowd of runners leaned toward the college's hilly terrain.

Bang!

As the women jumped off the line, Marie took an early and expected lead. Maureen and Joan Preston followed close behind. The North York girls were not only the youngest in the competition, but Maureen was the smallest.

As the pack reached the half-mile point, Maureen rushed ahead of the Washington, DC, favorite, and Joan followed, as if pulled by her teammate's momentum. The move broke Marie's resolve. Maureen powered up the inclines and around the corners of the course. Marie and the rest of the field fell farther and farther behind.

The Burnett hills training was paying dividends. The final half mile of the race was an extended hill of quad-busting steepness. Maureen charged up the path, crossing the finish line in nine minutes and 24.2 seconds. She had won the women's cross-country race with a decisive five-second lead.

Only when her breathing had returned to normal

and the buzz in her legs eased did the real gravity of what she'd done sink in. This was her first big race win. And it was also the attainment of something Brenda had told Maureen would happen years before: Maureen had powered her way to victory.

"Champions make champions," Sy would say. By competing against Brenda, day in and day out, Maureen became a stronger runner. They were at once each other's greatest competition and most loyal supporter. Brenda may have been sick, not at her best, and disappointed in her own placement, yet she was happy for her friend.

But before Maureen could truly celebrate her first big win, she had another race to compete in.

The event for twelve-year-old runners was co-ed. Of thirty-six entrants from Baltimore and beyond, Maureen and Joan Preston were the age group representatives from North York Track Club. Both were still recovering from their impressive finishes in the women's race (Joan had come in third).

Maureen's many months of training with the all-male Earl Haig Secondary School track team had given her plenty of practice of running with the opposite sex. The boys in this race, however, may not have been so accustomed to running with girls—and certainly not girls like Maureen.

With the crack of the starter pistol, the preteens took off.

Two boys from famously hilly Ithaca, New York, held the lead for the first three quarters of a mile.

Feeling buoyant from her performance in the earlier race, Maureen turned on the jets. Sprinting past the two New York boys up the final brutal hill, she claimed first place—and her second win of the day.

Maureen should have been euphoric. And she was, at first. She'd hit a personal milestone after years of dedication to the sport. Too bad someone had to go and ruin it.

Maureen got the news that her win in the women's cross-country race—the first race she had run that day—would not count. Her first-place finish would be scrubbed from the results and the second-place finisher would take home the prize. According to the American Amateur Athletic Union, the minimum age for an official event participant was fourteen. Maureen was two years shy. Even though she'd won, rules were rules. The girl should not have been in that race in the first place, the officials reasoned.

Maureen's buoyancy went flat. Her spirits sank. Not only was her championship medal stripped, but the North York Track Club also lost out on the first-place team prize in the first race since the scores from both

Maureen's and Joan's times were scrubbed from the team's point total.

Mean comments in newspapers, jabs about her sweatpants in public—those Maureen could handle, even if they made her feel uneasy and sometimes ashamed. But taking away a prize at a race? One that she'd earned outright? This was a moment Maureen learned that even people inside the running community, the ones who were supposed to be the most supportive, could stand against her.

Sy had a history of putting the girls in races that they were too young for as a way to challenge the rules. And he tended to keep the girls out of the drama of what boundaries he was pushing. His strategy allowed the girls to focus on running, but it didn't prepare them for disappointments such as this.

During the awards ceremony, Maureen took home the participant's trophy and first place in the twelve-year-old event, but not the medal for the women's cross-country race that she'd won. The mayor of Baltimore, so taken with Maureen's size and spirit after such an awful upset, lifted her up on his shoulders in a moment of spontaneous inspiration. The AAU rules lagged behind both the runners' abilities and the spectators' hearts.

"The mayor picked her up! She accelerated on the hill and passed her competitors! The audience loved her!"

Up in Canada, Margaret listened to Roger on the other end of the phone line. He was in Baltimore with Maureen, and she was at the shoe counter at Eaton's, a department store in Yorkdale Mall. Roger regaled her with the details of Maureen's latest races.

"The medal was stolen! Stolen! Even after she finished, she could have kept going!"

Roger used to leap through the kitchen's side door absolutely bubbling, delivering a thrilling recap of Maureen's races to Margaret. But now he delivered her Saturday race reports over the phone.

When Maureen started running, Margaret took care of the kids and managed the house. They were a family of modest means, and running—especially traveling to races—was expensive. In order to get Maureen to the events in Baltimore, Margaret started working three nights a week and on Saturdays at the Eaton's shoe counter.

"You're supposed to be selling shoes," a coworker would hiss, snapping Margaret back into the present.

But Margaret did not put down the phone. Her coworkers didn't understand the magnitude of what her daughter was doing or what Margaret was willingly sacrificing to protect it.

***

Margaret Wilton grew up in a cold industrial town on the Canadian side of Lake Superior during the Great Depression. As a child, she helped her family earn money by selling deer skins for twenty-five cents. She had four brothers and no sisters, so she learned early on how to hold her own. Margaret was very competitive. She grew up playing hockey, baseball, and football with her siblings, often playing against other groups of kids from the neighborhood. She made one catch in football that was legendary in her family. She remembers one of her brothers turning to her and saying, "Boy, am I ever glad to have you on my team." They'd play or skate outdoors together from morning until night, only coming inside once for lunch.

She met Roger Wilton at a church square dance when she was seventeen. They immediately hit it off. The next night, a Wednesday, they went to an amusement park together and then to the Palace Pier to dance. On Thursday, she went to a party in his honor, thrown by his aunt. And on Friday, his Air Force unit was deployed overseas to serve in the Second World War. They'd spent only three days together before he left. In the time he was away, Margaret and Roger wrote each other several times a week. In May of 1945, Roger returned to Canada for a short break before his next deployment to Japan was set to begin. While he was home, the war ended. Roger no longer had to leave. He and Margaret married a year later in June.

Margaret stopped playing sports when she was a kid, but when her daughter started running, the competitiveness from her childhood days reappeared. Margaret pulled Maureen aside at the Kitchener road races, pointing out that "there are maybe five kids out there that you gotta beat." Other runners remembered Margaret as a fierce supporter of her daughter. Support can take many forms. Sure, it's cheering, strategizing, and scoping out the competition. But it's also giving up something to make your daughter's passions possible. The adult version of hawking twenty-five-cent deer skins was forfeiting her spot at her daughter's Saturday races in order to fund them.

When Maureen was eleven or twelve years old, her parents sat her and her brothers down and asked which they would rather have: a pool in the backyard or a cottage on their land at Doe Lake. It was unanimous. All three kids wanted a cottage.

Margaret and Roger handled the construction of the water-access lakefront home themselves. It would have been hard diving into the construction only on weekends. But now Saturdays were filled with races for Maureen and hours at Eaton's for Margaret. Everything they had to do on their property in a week had to take place on a single day. They'd leave their house in North York before dawn early on Sunday mornings. They'd drive two and a half hours north to a town called Kearney, where they'd attend church services. When church was over, they'd drive for another half hour to get to their boat.

On some occasions, they'd bring Brenda, Jo-Ann, or another team member along. To make sure the girls got in their Sunday run, Roger might drop them off on a two-lane road, roughly five miles out from their boat. The girls would run past wild fields, dense clusters of pine, and the occasional farm. They'd meet the boat and the rest of the Wiltons on the shore.

Once Margaret and Roger loaded the craft with supplies and the kids, they'd cruise through the channel for thirty minutes until they reached their property. While the kids launched into the water off big rocks or ventured into the woods, Margaret and Roger would start building. It took them years to finish the simple structure that would house their family and friends. Maureen watched her parents, but especially her mother, in a near-constant state of work.

Margaret's and Roger's lives did bend around Maureen's running schedule, but the Wiltons' investment in Maureen's running paid them all dividends. For Maureen, the club gave her passion and purpose. The people she met there became her community. She shared an almost sisterly closeness with Carol, she and Jo-Ann became the tightest of friends, and Brenda understood every step in Maureen's journey as an internationally competitive runner. *These* were her people. With them, she could be her true self: obsessive, silly, fiercely loyal, and supportive. She even struck up a friendship with a parent in the club named Gord Sim, who used to give her a ride home on his motorcycle.

"Dairy Queen?" Mr. Sim would ask, wearing head-to-toe black leathers over his running clothes after practice. Maureen would pull on a helmet and hop on the back of his small motorcycle.

"Chocolate-dipped cone, please," she'd say at the counter, always ordering her favorite. They'd eat their ice creams and then Mr. Sim would ferry her home.

Parents in the club took turns driving the girls to races. Through their kids, the older cohorts became quite close as well. An adult running club spun off from the North York Track Club. Mr. and Mrs. Sim, Sheila Meharg's parents, Maureen's priest (which was only slightly strange for Maureen), and Coach Sy himself were all members. If not otherwise occupied with a meet, the girls joined the adults for their long weekend-morning runs.

***

For most of the girls, the decision to join a running club became so much more than the sum of its practices. It was certainly this way for Carol, though her experience was quite different from the other kids', who had two parents at home and comfortable finances. Carol's mother couldn't contribute time or money to her daughter's extracurriculars; she was too busy with work and raising five daughters as a single parent. Carol's mother did her best for the family—and Carol knew that—but the price was that Carol didn't get a lot of one-on-one time with her mother.

At the track, Sy worked with her. And under his instruction, Carol became a strong contender in long-distance running contests throughout Canada. During the national age-class championship one-mile race in Ottawa, Carol was behind. To spectators, it didn't look like she was going to be able to catch the front-runner. Then, in the final stretch, and despite the mile being her least-favorite distance, she found an extra gear. Carol surged ahead of her competition and won the race. It was a spectacular finish and a big moment for Carol. She went home with a trophy! But it was what happened afterward that meant the most to her.

When she returned to practice the next week, she expected the usual Monday-afternoon interval torture. But instead, Sy rounded up the team in a portable classroom on the Earl Haig campus and asked Carol to stand up next to him. Sy praised her efforts in front of the rest of the team for what felt like half an hour.

For another runner, this might have felt like an appreciated pat on the back, the kind of thing you get from parents or grandparents when they're really proud. But for Carol, this feeling she got was entirely new. It was the first time anyone had ever acknowledged her personally as someone special—and Sy did it in front of all her friends in the club. She held on to his every word, knowing it was a moment she would never forget.

Maureen and the other girls were oblivious to many of the challenges facing Carol. But in some ways, that was a refreshing change. With the team, she wasn't a kid with a difficult family situation and financial struggles; she was a strong long-distance runner, a valued teammate, and a friend.

The team also gave Carol space to dream. As she competed in more races and against girls all over Canada and the United States, she imagined a greater future for herself in running. She was a strong athlete, but she wanted to be the best. Carol wanted to be an Olympian. It was a goal that helped motivate her through tortuous miles and searing hill climbs. But there was a catch. Carol was a long-distance runner, and the Olympics didn't offer any long-distance running events for women. (In the 1960 games, women could once again race the 800, but that was the longest event.) Carol's hope was that one day soon, before her window closed, that would change.

To prepare, she and the other girls on the team subjected themselves to every Sy workout and adopted each and every one of his strategies, without ever seriously questioning them. That allegiance to his often extreme training plan worked out better for some girls than others.

10

Sy told all the girls to meet at his house on Friday right after school. From there, the plan was to load into his aging red Pontiac Laurentian station wagon and drive eight and a half hours south, all the way to a race in Maryland.

When Jo-Ann and her father arrived, Jo-Ann joined her teammates, jumping around excitedly.

Sy heaved the runner's luggage into the trunk.

Then Jo-Ann's father spotted the tires. They were balding, with barely a groove left to grip the road.

Jo-Ann's father owned a distribution business for Imperial Oil, and he had two oil trucks and employed two drivers. He knew that Sy's station wagon tires were not fit for the trip.

But Sy took home only a teacher's salary. And in addition to Brenda, he had a wife and three other daughters at home to support. Time was something Sy could give—and he gave lots of it to the team—but shelling out money for a brand-new set of wheels? That was a tougher problem for Sy to solve.

Jo-Ann's father stepped in.

"Take my card."

Sy's wife took the car and the credit card to a nearby mechanic, where a brand-new set of tires was installed that afternoon.

The team was delayed, but not derailed. Once Sy got back with the car, Maureen and the rest of the girls claimed their seats. (Maureen's personal favorite was the rear-facing rumble seat in the very back.) Sy turned on his headlights and headed south under cool, dark Ontario skies.

On the drive over the finger of land between Lake Ontario to the north and Lake Erie to the south, they sang the classics ("Ninety-nine Bottles of Beer on the Wall" obviously and "On Top of Spaghetti, All Covered with Cheese"), listened to music, and played a game to see who could touch all the car's ceiling panels the fastest. (Even off the track, Maureen liked a competition.) Finally, with the road rumbling below them and many miles ahead, Maureen and the rest of the girls drifted off to sleep five across on folded-down seats like sardines. Sy was at the wheel, driving in the United States now, and kept going . . .

Until he slowed the station wagon to a stop.

"Everybody out!" said Sy. "This is a famous bridge and you're going to run across it."

The girls blinked their heavy eyelids and looked

around. Night and nothing. It was who-knows-what o'clock, and what bridge was he talking about? They'd already lost the details.

The girls tentatively opened the doors and climbed out of the car into darkness. There was no one on the road and it was hard to see anything beyond it. But there was a bridge in front of them, and in what had become a relatively normal ritual when they encountered something noteworthy during their travels, Sy wanted them to run it. And the girls listened.

When they reached the other side, Sy stopped the car, and the girls settled back in. The whole crew assumed their positions: Sy at the wheel and the girls back to sleep.

***

Top 40 hits echoed through the North York Centennial Arena—chartbusters such as "Hang On Sloopy," "Turn! Turn! Turn!," "Day Tripper," and "I Got You (I Feel Good)."

Even though the melodies sounded like they were being broadcast in the belly of a metal boat, the music did add lightness to the hard practice. As did the sight of figure skaters below and the sounds of their metal blades cutting into the ice. This was the club's home during the winter training months, when snow blanketed Earl Haig's outdoor track. High above the skaters, on a concrete indoor track that ringed the building between the lower and upper sections of seating, rumbled the North York Track Club.

Instead of offering a little give or spring underfoot like a cinder track, the concrete surface course fought back against every footfall. Many of the girls ran in the six-dollar Tiger running shoes supplied by Sy, which in those days were thin soled and offered no substantial padding or protection to the foot. Over time that constant punch from the track caused many runners injury and pain, particularly from shin splints. But if any North York runner complained of such an ailment, Sy would reply, without looking up from his clipboard: "Do you want to win?"

Every girl on the team had the same answer. "Yes!"

"Then get on the track."

Sy was firm yet fair. Funny, affable, good with both the parents and the kids—and not a yeller during practice or during competitions. For Maureen and many of the other girls, Sy was someone they respected and trusted. If he told them to run 440 yards twenty times on a track that blistered their feet and beat up their legs, they did it. A banked wooden indoor track that was all corners? They ran that, too. And as a team, they were winning. Brenda came in first at Maple Leaf

Gardens; Jo-Ann won the thirteen-and-under half-mile event in Aurora; Maureen came in second at a mile-and-a-quarter event in Hamilton. At these events North York Track Club often took home a team prize.

Maureen had good reason to trust Sy's coaching.

She knew Sy thought a lot of her, and she didn't want to disappoint him.

Neither did Sheila, who came to practice even though she was quite sick. Sy wanted her to continue—and she would have done it—had her father not gently extracted her.

On another occasion, Jo-Ann attempted the workout even though she couldn't put any weight on her right heel. She was limping on that banked wooden track—the club's other winter training place—only able to put her right toes on the ground. Her heels had been killing her, but Sy practiced a kill-it-to-cure-it philosophy. And so Jo Ann went out for another lap. It looked less like running and more like an impression of a wounded animal.

"Mr. Mah," Jo-Ann's dad said, watching his daughter attempt to run. "It looks like she's having some difficulty with her feet."

Jo-Ann was tough, but her father didn't see how limping around the track constituted training. She looked like someone who needed help, not tough love. He pulled her out of practice and got her an appointment with an orthopedic surgeon.

After examining her legs and feet—and listening to lots of chatter about wanting to get back to the track and back to racing—the surgeon gave Jo-Ann a diagnosis: Achilles tendinitis. The tendons on the backs of her legs that connect the calf muscles to her heel bones had been pushed too far. Keep going and the badly scarred and inflamed tendons could tear. The surgeon gave Jo-Ann a stern warning, "Either you're going to take one year off or you will be getting casts up to your knees."

Jo-Ann reluctantly took a yearlong break. Or rather, she took the year off *from running*. To stay in shape while her Achilles healed, she swam competitively. And then, as soon as she got the medical clearance, she came back.

Maureen also pushed herself hard, but she rarely got injured. She had shin splints for a while and later a bruised heel, but neither of these things sidelined her. One reason she may have avoided injury was that she put in a lot of slow, easy miles on her own as part of her training.

On days when she didn't have practice, Maureen ran by herself, no matter the weather conditions. She ran in the heat and the freezing rain. When they traveled to meets, Maureen would often feel a little disappointed that the hours in the car meant missing a run. So when Sy suggested jogging rather than driving to local races, Maureen said yes and told her mom.

"We're jogging down as part of the warm-up."

"What!" exclaimed Margaret. "That's ten miles."

Maureen knew what she was in for. And she'd never turn down a run.

The girls developed an amazing toughness. In one race during the Canadian Women's Cross-Country Championships in Vancouver (a race the club had to raise money to attend), Brenda fell on the course after being pushed by another runner. Because there were 110 runners racing on the very crowded track, it's not surprising that a spike on the underside of a passing sprinter's shoe pierced Brenda's leg. She was down and visibly bleeding. An assistant coach tried to call her off the course, thinking her race was over.

As she scrambled to her feet and resumed running, she said to the coach, "I didn't come all the way to Vancouver to watch." Brenda submitted herself for medical attention and some stitches only after the race was over.

If this seems extreme for ten-, eleven-, twelve-, and thirteen-year-olds, that's because coaching kids competitively—especially girls of this age—was a brand-new endeavor. Sy had to weave through the public's misconceptions about girls and distance running, most of which revolved around the harm that it would do to them. Sy could see the talent, strength, and stamina of even the youngest club members, and he advocated for them in the papers and by testing the limits of the distances and minimum ages that the Amateur Athletic Union would allow. And he made sure the girls were ready for their events by keeping them on a rigorous training schedule. But during that process, some members of the team did get injured.

Sy's high standards as a coach owed much to an older coach in the Toronto area named Lloyd Percival, who oversaw the training of the remarkable runner (and often North York Track Club competitor) Roberta Picco as well as the Don Mills Track Club.

By the time he knew Maureen, Lloyd was in his fifties. Maureen would say hello to the bespectacled coach at events. North York competed against the Don Mills club with relative frequency, so the coaches and runners were friendly.

But Lloyd was more than a coach. He was also the founder and director of the Fitness Institute and a researcher, forever pushing for the advancement of the sport. He was an early and vocal public advocate for women's running and a sharp critic of the Amateur Athletic Union. When Brenda and Maureen were banned from this or that competition for being under the age minimum of fourteen, Lloyd spoke up: "The AAU age limit is based solely on uneducated opinion," he argued, countering much of what officials worried about at the time. "There is no medical evidence to show damage to youngsters' hearts or internal organs provided there is no basic weakness."

He was a respected voice who had been interested in sports and coaching techniques since he was a kid.

When Lloyd was a teenager, he played a lot of sports—boxing, basketball, hockey, baseball, tennis, gymnastics—and played them well. So well in fact that when he was sixteen years old, he made it all the way to the final match of the Canadian Open Junior Tennis Championship. In this final competition, Lloyd believed he would win. His opponent was the best junior tennis player in the United States, but Lloyd was stronger, quicker, and in better shape. Yet much to Lloyd's surprise, he lost. After the game was over, he confronted his opponent's coach: *How could this have possibly happened?* The answer: "Coaching." It changed the trajectory of his life.

As Lloyd grew up, he became a coach himself for athletes in a variety of sports, especially hockey and track. In track and field, up until this point, there was nothing even approaching a unified theory about how to produce the best athletes. What coaches had was a tangle of traditions and opinions. There was little attention paid to what athletes ate, how they warmed up, or new techniques in training. Lloyd saw all these areas as dials to twist—things he could calibrate to produce exceptional athletes.

But first, he needed to research the methods and practices of track-and-field coaches around Canada and the United States. So he wrote to them, sending them questionnaires asking about how the coaches trained their athletes. This kind of information gathering had never been done before. Lloyd figured that collecting and sharing this knowledge would not only help the sport, but also raise Canada's track-and-field profile around the world.

And then Lloyd went even further. Years after the first round of surveys went out, Lloyd established a track-and-field testing group. It was a place where he could work with athletes to test how varied nutrition and training techniques affected performance.

One of his biggest revelations observing athletes: What they eat matters. His favorite items for an athlete were yogurt, oranges for their vitamin C, and dried figs because of their iron content. He also introduced Canada to two training techniques that would be key to national running success: fartleks—a funny-sounding

Swedish word that means "speed play"—and interval training, which means running fast, short distances with short breaks in between.

Lloyd's work was the genesis of how intervals became a Sy Mah track practice staple. But more important for Maureen and for Sy, Lloyd also saw the potential of Canadian women in the sport and the opportunity to transform them into competitors on the world stage.

When Lloyd started doing this research, the AAU believed that running was "unacceptably masculine." In other words, women shouldn't do it. So Lloyd challenged the problem from a number of different angles. He wrote about how women should run, he made a club where women could run, he recruited women to run, he hosted races to provide more opportunities for women to compete, and he staged events aimed at expanding what the sport's regulating bodies believed women could do, particularly in long distances. When people disagreed with him, he offered scientifically backed armor: the data from his testing group.

By the time he recruited Roberta Picco from her school's track team in 1964, Lloyd had already retired from coaching several times over. He'd written a series of books aimed at improving performance in sports— *How to Play Better Hockey, How to Play Better Basketball,*

How to Be a Track and Field Champion—and he'd tested his theories on athletes all over the country.

Roberta was tall, strong, and, with the influence of Lloyd's coaching, unstoppable.

Sy had benefited from Lloyd's decades of work on coaching and sports, even following his example when it came to pushing regulatory boundaries for the betterment of his runners. With Sy's coaching, Brenda and Maureen were fast. But Roberta was always faster.

Roberta had emigrated from Italy to Canada when she was ten. Her father had gotten a job with the Canadian Pacific Railway four years earlier, and she and her mom moved to Canada to join him. When she arrived, her parents settled into an Italian neighborhood. Initially Roberta didn't speak any English, which made getting along with the kids at school challenging.

One thing the newcomer had in her favor: She was fast. At recess, she played tag with the boys. And pretty quickly she realized that not only was she a good runner—but it was something she really enjoyed.

Roberta was fifteen years old when she started training with the Don Mills Track Club. Lloyd pushed her hard. But like Maureen and Carol, running offered her benefits beyond athletic success. She made friends with other runners. When Roberta traveled for meets, she did so as a representative of Canada. On the road, they ate Canadian food, and when the club traveled, she traveled with Canadian teammates. For the first time since she'd arrived in the country, she didn't feel like an immigrant, she felt Canadian.

Running helped her fit into one community, but it made it harder for her at home. Her parents weren't supportive and wouldn't drive her to practice, so in order to attend workouts, Roberta had to spend an hour and a half commuting each way. There was time in her day for school and the running club, and that was about it. But her dedication to Lloyd's training paid off. Roberta quickly became one of the most powerful runners, not just in Toronto, but in all of Canada. She cherished the medals and trophies she brought home. They were proof of not only her hard work, but her warm welcome in the running community.

***

When Maureen got into bed at her home every night, a few miles east of Roberta's house, she, too, was surrounded by trophies. Her room was small, painted a pale mauve. In it, her parents had installed a high shelf that ringed the room. And on that high shelf were more and more little gold statues—usually with male figures, sometimes female—atop every shape of wooden pedestal, most with a little gold rectangular name plate at the base engraved with, at the very least, the year and the place Maureen finished.

This growing collection was a visible symbol of how important running was to her and also how accomplished she'd become. Maureen had taken home trophies all over Canada, from Vancouver on Canada's west coast to Ottawa and meets in the eastern United States. Her name appeared in local papers almost every weekend, and news of her efforts on the track spread through running communities far beyond her own. She was called "little Moe" in these accounts, as well as "petite and pretty Maureen Wilton" and "spunky Maureen." To her team, she was "Mighty Moe," the nickname she liked best.

The training, the hard work: it was all worth it, even more so because there seemed to be no limit to what she was capable of.

11

As Maureen's career bloomed, so did girls' track and field across North America. In the United States, clubs popped up like wildflowers in seemingly random towns in every region of the country. The San Diego Mission Belles, Will's Spikettes of Sacramento, Valley of the Sun Track Club of Phoenix, Seattle Olympic, the Hoosier Track Club of Indianapolis, Nan Demuth's Finger Lakes Track Club, the Astronettes of Yonkers, and on and on.

In 1966, women's cross-country races appeared in places like Indiana, Florida, central New York, and Pennsylvania for the first time. In some parts of the country—Albuquerque, Phoenix, and Kalispell, Montana—there were running clubs for women, but no races nearby. Yet. But things were beginning to change. In New York and Michigan there were enough clubs and meets to keep girls busy almost the entire year.

A cadre of coaches around the country, willing to donate a little of their time after school to oversee workouts, started recruiting girls with a fire to race.

They weren't hard to find.

Dick Beyst went looking in 1965. He started running indoor meets in a gymnasium near south Detroit, Michigan, for girls as young as seven. Girls didn't have to sign up for the club to compete. They just needed to show up.

But once they did, Beyst did everything he could to convince them to stay. He knocked on the door of Jacki Ford, a feisty fourteen-year-old girl he'd seen run in one of his small gym meets.

When she answered, he got straight to the point: "Want to run in a state meet?"

Jacki, never one to turn down competition, agreed—despite her parents' disapproval. She stuck with Beyst, becoming one of the founding members of the Lincoln Park Parkettes. To Jacki, it felt like the group doubled in size every week. It grew to sixty girls ranging from seven years old on up to eighteen.

Beyst treated Jacki and the rest of the team with a seriousness that she'd never experienced before. He was strict, demanding in practice that they push themselves to exhaustion. During workouts, he'd yell, "What *don't* you want to do today?"

Girls who didn't know any better would respond, "Run all out."

"On the line," he'd yell back. "You're going to all run a mile as fast as you can."

In practice, Beyst didn't care if the girls looked "feminine" or "ladylike." He'd make them crab walk—supporting their body weight with their hands and legs, stomachs facing up—on a dirt hill peppered with rocks. He had them trot quarter-mile laps on the track with other girls on their backs. Every so often, he'd yell, "Push-up position!"

The girls would drop onto their hands and feet, their backs as straight as boards.

"Who is going to be the first to quit?" he'd ask.

He wanted his girls to be the best they could. He wanted them to be strong.

Jacki loved every minute of it. Finally, someone wasn't treating her like a doll. At track, she was surrounded by young women and a coach who didn't mind breaking a sweat, who wanted to *win* something. At home, she didn't get the same support. Her aunt asked her what she planned to do with all those medals when she grew up. Her father told her running around in circles was silly.

But Beyst was cognizant of what his coaching tactics might look like to critics. At track meets, he urged his athletes to smile when they crossed the finish—no matter how painful the race felt. When newspaper reporters flocked, he made sure the Parkettes answered with grace and restraint. Whatever he was doing, it worked. Jacki and the Parkettes started winning countrywide meets.

Other track teams went to greater lengths to get attention. In Abilene, Texas, a secretary named Margaret Ellison with a strawberry-blond hairdo to match her sizable ego founded the Texas Track Club. Gilbert Rogin, a nationally known writer for *Sports Illustrated*, traveled south to follow the group.

The Texas Track Club, Rogin wrote, was famous for two reasons: "its athletic achievements and the uncommon beauty of its girls, who compete in dazzling uniforms, elaborate makeup, and majestic hairdos. These hairdos, which are either bouffant or flip if at all possible, may not be aerodynamically sound and may be 'out' east of the Hudson, but they are an unqualified sensation at a track meet."

Three members of the club, their hair sufficiently poofed and their lipstick glistening red, appeared on the cover of the magazine on April 20, 1964. They were the first female track athletes featured on the front of *Sports Illustrated* in the publication's history.

The fact that this team, presented to look more like pinup models than actual athletes, earned national recognition rankled other female track-and-field athletes.

The article inside made them furious.

Here's a sampling:

In one sense, the Texas Track Club has done more to promote women's track in the U.S. than if its members had, say, won the national AAU championships. (In fact, they finished twelfth last year, with a third in the 440-yard relay and the 220-yard low hurdles and a sixth in the 220-yard dash.) After the age of 10, American girls generally lose interest in running—it is unbecoming and too far out. And American boys generally lose interest in the few girls who take up the sport, the popular belief being that they look like Olive Oyl or Tugboat Annie. The Texas Track Club, however, has shown that you can be beautiful and still run the 100 in 10.9. Because of this delightful anomaly, its members have been a hit.

As female athletes and their coaches knew, beauty wasn't the reason women's track ignited across the country. It was the serious competition.

Overall, attendance at women's meets climbed. Instead of a dozen or so girls attending one event, a regional championship in California could draw some three hundred entrants—a shockingly steep climb from years prior. Bob Hyten, the coach of the Ozark Track Club in Saint Louis, declared that 1966 was the year "women's cross country pass[ed] from its infancy into adolescence."

As part of this growth, women's track finally got its own magazine: *Cinderbelle: News and Views of Women's Track and Field*.

Behind the creamsicle-orange cover with curvy script, girls learned about their competition. Coaches could compare training methods. And readers of all ages, genders, and ability levels could write in to complain about the still-persistent inequalities.

Most of those complaints were fired directly at America's Amateur Athletic Union, the bloated body of officials—mostly men—in charge of organizing track meets across the country.

In 1966, a man named Herb Stockman published a several-thousand-word diatribe against the AAU. He'd recently been kicked out of the organization after serving as the Girls Age Group Track and Field Chairman, tasked with refining and improving the rules governing the length and age limits of events for the youngest competitors. He recommended that girls thirteen years old and younger be allowed to race up to a mile. His letter documents a meeting where a few of his colleagues vehemently disagreed.

He wrote, "Alvin Lloyd gets up in front of the committee in Hawaii and says how many young girls he has seen at the finish of cross-country races in California 'FOAMING AT THE MOUTH' and that this type of running is bad for young girls.

"Now just who is Alvin Lloyd?" the letter continues. "Is he a COACH? NO. Is he a parent of a young track athlete? NO. Is he an authority on the physiology of young athletes? NO."

The AAU listened to Alvin. Then they booted Herb.

Still, in what used to be a desert for women's running, clubs were appearing. And those clubs hosted races, races that the local papers covered. Those articles sparked more interest, and got more girls running, which led to bigger competitions. Girls pushed each other to run faster, run farther. Records fell rapidly until it wasn't the speed that marked the limits of girls' potential, it was the old and arbitrary rules that blocked them from running long. The girls and the coaches who tested those boundaries were doing something that women had never been allowed to do before—in fact *still* weren't allowed to do, but did anyways. They took steps to run in new places, new races, and longer distances. It was like forcing their way onto the moon without support from ground control.

The name of one of those girls, closest to that

uncharted moon territory, started pinging throughout clubs around the country.

"You don't want to run this workout?" Dick Beyst would ask Jacki Ford and the Parkettes. "I hear little Maureen Wilton did ten quarters yesterday. What are you going to do today?"

12

Toronto's largest public park, High Park, is pretty in early April. Leafing branches hang over the groomed paths, making it feel like you are wandering through a deep-green tunnel. For the most part, winter has finished—though cold winds can still pierce through the new foliage, whipping off giant Lake Ontario just to the south.

The park is a few weeks out from dazzling. In 1959, the Japanese ambassador to Canada gifted the city two thousand Sakura cherry trees. They were planted on a road that cuts through the middle of the park. For eleven and a half months of the year, the trees look like any other, until the perfect amount of sunlight, moisture, and warmth seeps into their branches. When that happens, for just two weeks a year, thousands of brilliantly white and pink blossoms explode from their branches. The trees look like fireworks, frozen in time.

The show usually happens near the first week in May.

At the start of the Toronto Spring Road Races on April 15, 1967, Sy Mah stood near one of those cherry trees. It had scraggly branches and just a hint of tiny green flower buds.

Sy was there for a weekend packed with events showcasing top Canadian road-racing talent. In the main event that morning, the men completed a ten-mile course.

Mah had registered Maureen for the women's 1.5-mile open race.

As far as race strategy goes, the 1.5 mile might just be one of the trickiest distances in running. It exists in a weird middle area between the shorter races that favor sprinters and the longer races that endurance runners love.

A sprinter wants everyone in her race to go as fast as possible in order for the winner to know that she is the fastest of all. A distance runner is more cruel. She wants everyone to go hard at the beginning of a race so her competitors all feel dead at the end. The winner knows she can survive pain better than anyone.

Sy Mah scanned the starting line from his spot by the trees. He could see one of the region's best natural distance runners line up next to one of the region's best sprinters. Next to them stood Maureen. He hoped she could keep up.

This was going to be a thrilling test of strategy.

***

Just don't make the same mistake. Don't make the same mistake, Maureen thought to herself.

She shook out her legs and scanned across the grassy field inside the park. She could see Roberta Picco warming up. Roberta had a graceful, confident stride and powerful lungs that could carry those legs seemingly forever. She was a distance runner with the speed of a sprinter. The lethal combination meant Roberta led races from the front, rarely giving up her position. In some races, Maureen was so far behind Roberta that she couldn't see her finish.

Maureen also spotted Cathy Griffith, the formidable sprinter from the Toronto Striders. Cathy specialized in the 440 and 880, distances where speed mattered a lot more than endurance. Maureen could hang with Cathy during the start of races, but she just wasn't fast enough when it mattered—during the final, painful surge across the finish line.

Maureen had never defeated either one of them.

Would Maureen be closer this time? Would she at least be able to see Roberta slingshot toward the finish with that unbeatable speed? *Maybe*, Maureen thought. As long as she didn't mess up like last time.

Last time was just two weeks previous, during a series of road races put on by the local Gladstone Athletic Club at a different park just ten minutes away.

The distance was the same—1.5 miles. As was the chief competition—Cathy and Roberta. When the starter's pistol had fired, Roberta steamrolled to the front, asserting the pace. It felt blistering to Maureen. She had attempted to stick with Roberta and leave Cathy behind. But Maureen started out too fast, and in the end, she couldn't keep up. Roberta won in seven minutes and forty-nine seconds. Cathy followed, finishing in seven minutes and fifty-five seconds. Then came Maureen, lagging behind in eight minutes and five seconds. Third place was fine and all—it got your name in the paper—but Maureen knew she could do better.

So at the start line of the Toronto Spring Road Races, she had a plan. If Roberta was going to charge from the starting line with a scorching pace while Cathy followed, then Maureen would let them. She was going to bide her time. She'd stalk Roberta and Cathy as they tired each other out. In this rematch, Maureen was going to attack from behind.

***

The pistol fired and two girls streaked to the front. Sy could see Roberta and Cathy, both of whom towered over Maureen. A large gap began to open up between the two leaders and his runner: ten meters, then twenty, then forty.

What is Maureen doing? Maybe she's tired. Maybe it's just not her day.

The girls disappeared around a corner. When your runner is losing, any coach would mull over the tactics. *Does she need a tweak in training? Is she putting in too many miles? Too few? Will she ever rise to the level of her formidable competitors?*

After six or so minutes, Sy heard yelps in the distance. The course would soon bring the runners back into view. He checked his watch. The race was about to finish, and judging by the noise along the course it was close. Probably another Cathy-and-Roberta battle.

"Look at that little girl go!" someone shouted.

A tiny lithe frame appeared under the canopy of expectant cherry tree branches. Shoulder to shoulder, Maureen and Roberta charged to the finish.

Maureen had executed her plan perfectly. For three-quarters of a mile, she let Cathy and Roberta fight for position and pace. Then, feeling strong, Maureen surged. She passed Cathy with a mile to go. Her eyes locked on Roberta's short black hair. Every step, Mighty Moe came closer, until she couldn't see the jet-black strands anymore, just trees, a road, and in the distance, a finish line.

The homestretch passed in a whir of limbs, gasps for air with the cramping twinge of lactic acid building in the muscles, and the cheers from a surprised crowd. Maureen was not supposed to be this close to Canadian running champion Roberta Picco.

"Did that little girl win?" the course judge at the mile mark had huffed to the finish to ask. "I thought for sure she would win. She looked so great."

No. Maureen didn't win. She lost by a heartbeat—1.3 seconds, the closest she'd ever come to beating Roberta.

When reporters gathered around Sy Mah to get his thoughts on the race, he didn't speak about the defeat. He didn't see it as one. Instead, he saw it as proof that under the right conditions, Maureen could explode into something stunning.

"I wish there was a women's marathon race. Maureen seems to have no limit to her endurance," he told the reporters.

The cherry blossoms still needed a few more weeks before they would bloom.

PART II

THE RACE

13

"Do you want to run a marathon?"

Sy Mah had ambled across the grassy field next to Earl Haig to ask Maureen the question after practice. It had been two days since she had nearly defeated Roberta Picco—a fact Maureen still could hardly believe. She'd tussled with one of Canada's best female distance runners and had almost come out on top.

"What's a marathon?" she asked as she stretched out her legs.

"It's a long run," he answered.

"How long?" she responded casually. In practice sessions, she'd already completed workouts of fifteen miles in one shot. Maureen could run long.

"Twenty-six point two miles," Mah said.

The first time most people hear the actual distance of a marathon, they flinch. *"Twenty-six point two miles,"* they say incredulously—dragging out the word *miles* for emphasis to make sure they've heard correctly. "That's farther than I *drive* most days," they might add. And it's true. Accelerating down the freeway—at a speed where the surroundings begin to blur—it would take a driver about thirty minutes to go all 26.2 miles. If Maureen started running south from Earl Haig, she'd hit Toronto, then Lake Ontario, and still not be even halfway done with 26.2 miles.

She didn't flinch when she heard the distance.

"I'll do it," she said, not sounding the least bit concerned with what she'd just committed to.

Sy had always handled her racing schedule. Weekly, he'd let her know what races were coming. He'd already asked her to get on airplanes and jet around the country. He'd driven her hundreds of miles himself. He'd asked her to compete in two races in one day. He'd asked her to run against boys and chase down future Olympians who were years older than her. So asking her if she wanted to run a marathon seemed normal.

Sure, a marathon was long. A bit longer than she had ever run before. But it was just a race. Just something to finish—another challenge dreamed up by Sy. Maureen didn't ask him the name of the race. She trusted her coach. She didn't even think to ask him if she was allowed to run it.

A marathon, Maureen thought, was no big deal.

***

The first-ever marathon, as legend goes, happened because of war.

Roughly 2,500 years ago, a man named King Darius the First was furious.

Despite being one of the world's most powerful men, controlling a vast empire called Persia that stretched from modern-day Turkey to China, Darius was mad about a lot of things. He was mad that he wasn't a direct descendant of the throne, so he murdered the man who was. He was mad that subjects on the outskirts of his empire began to revolt, so he sent his armies to quash them. And he was mad that the Greeks, a much smaller empire across the Aegean Sea, had jumped in to help the rebellion.

Darius wanted to destroy the Greeks.

He sent twenty thousand men in ships across the narrow waters between the two empires to get the job done. The frightening force landed near the town of Marathon in Greece. They outnumbered the Greek army nearly two to one. Miltiades, the general of the Greek army, desperately needed help if he was going to protect the land and stop Darius's forces. The general decided he would ask the Spartans, legendary warriors who ruled roughly 150 miles south of Marathon, for help. He needed someone to deliver the plea. Speed was essential. The fastest way to travel over the dusty, narrow, and hilly trails? On foot.

Ancient historians claim that a Greek messenger

named Pheidippides managed to run over brutal terrain to complete the journey in less than twenty-four hours—an astonishing feat of endurance. But he wasn't done. The Spartans let him know they couldn't come and help in the battle. They were preoccupied with celebrating a religious festival. So Pheidippides turned around to rush back to Marathon to deliver the disappointing answer.

It wasn't needed. The Greeks, with far fewer numbers, crushed the Persians. Miltiades's army lost only 192 men to the 6,400 killed in Darius's army.

Now someone needed to deliver the glorious news to the worried leaders in Athens—a twenty-five-mile journey. Pheidippides, presumably exhausted from his previous exploits, was called upon again.

No one knows precisely how long it took him, but what's certain is that it was a gut-wrenching journey. The most likely route took him over hills and exposed terrain. It was probably scorching hot. His mind was likely waging war against his body. He had to compel aching, failing muscles to move forward. He had a message to deliver that would change the course of history. The legend says he staggered into the Acropolis at the end of the road and uttered a single word: *"Nenikhkamen!"*

"We have won!" the ancient Greek word means.

Then he collapsed and died. The first marathon literally killed a man.

Historically accurate or not (a single man completing 326 miles in three bursts over a short period of time is probably not), the story of Pheidippides ignited the imaginations of athletes for centuries. In 1896, Greece organized the first modern-day Olympics. As part of the competition, they hosted a footrace from the battlefield of Marathon to the Panathenaic Stadium in Athens to re-create Pheidippides's legendary run. Seventeen men started the race. Only nine finished. A local named Spiridon Louis won, instantly becoming a national hero.

A newspaper in Athens reported at the time that a Greek woman named Melpomene tried to enter the race. In a trial run, she'd completed the course in four and a half hours. Despite proving she could do it, she was denied a spot because "the Games competition format was for men only."

It stayed that way for more than three-quarters of a century.

The marathon enticed men from around the world. It was challenging, something you could brag about while sipping wine or cognac in a bar after the finish. The fact that its origins were rooted in death and war and Greek mythology helped. Races mimicking the distance of the

Greek route (roughly twenty-five miles) cropped up in New York City, Boston, Paris, and Saint Louis. In 1908 at the London Olympics, the course was modified so that a princess could see the start at Windsor Castle and the Queen could see the finish in the stadium in London. There were 26.2 miles between the two royals. That length stuck as the new marathon standard.

Because the marathon was a uniquely challenging distance and often occurred on desolate roads between major cities, men cheated—often. In the 1896 race, the third-place finisher was disqualified after he was caught taking a vehicle for part of the course. At the 1904 Olympics in Saint Louis, an American named Fred Lorz won gold—until officials discovered he'd ridden in a car for eleven miles.

Though it wasn't considered cheating, men tried to ingest anything they could to gain an advantage (well, nearly anything except water—which in those days was viewed as a performance inhibitor). In that same 1904 race where Lorz cheated, other runners slurped whiskey and took rat poison, thinking the concoction would preserve their energy. Spiridon Louis, the winner of the first Olympic Marathon, chomped on orange slices a few miles from the finish. The third-place finisher relied on wine.

The distance presented uncharted territory as an

athletic challenge, and athletes had only just begun fig-
uring out the ideal way to complete it, tinkering with
training, hydration, and pace. One thing remained constant, though. As times dropped and the popularity of
the distance spread, women were always excluded.

It was rarely explicitly said that a woman shouldn't
or couldn't finish a marathon, just like it was never
explicitly said that a dog shouldn't or couldn't drive a
car. To many people in the early and mid-1900s, both
would have seemed equally preposterous.

The naysayers focused on the fact that women were
physically different and thus should not do the same
things as men.

The founder of the modern Olympic Games, a
wealthy Frenchman named Pierre de Coubertin, once
said that women competing was "impractical, uninteresting, ungainly, and, I do not hesitate to add, improper."

In a 1931 issue of the *Detroit Free Press*, a "well known
beauty specialist" named Elizabeth Arden said, "Women
should not exercise as men do." The article continues,
saying, "Most exercises for women are performed in the
lying position." And having bulging muscles and over-
exertion won't make women "beautiful."

One of America's most famous strongmen, Charles
Atlas, was a bit more blunt in 1936. When asked if
women should exercise, he responded, "Pretty soon

they have a beard. That is bad. Women should not exercise to the extremes."

A marathon is *definitely* extreme, and it is the literal opposite of working out while lying down. With rumors about the threat of facial hair, the loss of beauty, and the inability to have children, why would a woman risk it?

14

Bushes can be an excellent place to hide if you want
to break the rules. You'll need them to be tall and thick
enough to disguise your baggy gray sweatshirt and
sunshine-bright blond hair. Preferably, the branches
won't have thorns.

On December 14, 1963, a woman named Merry Lepper found the perfect bushes to crouch behind on a road
near Veterans Memorial Park in Culver City, California.
She was twenty years old—tall and skinny—and a vet-
erinary student with an undying love for horses.

She huddled next to her friend and training partner,
Lyn Carman, behind the wall of green, hoping none of
the sixty or so men stretching on the pavement not far
away would notice. The two were about to break a rule
no known North American woman had ever broken.
They were about to run a marathon.

Merry was nervous. She'd already lied to her parents about how far she was planning on running that
day. They knew she liked to run, so heading to a race
on a weekend was normal. But 26.2 miles? Merry feared
telling them would cause trouble. She, of course, had

reasons to worry. She knew race officials wouldn't like her showing up. She especially knew people watching the race would give her a hard time. Having run track since high school, then working her way up to longer runs on the streets of San Bernardino, a town seventy miles west of this park, she'd experienced the taunts yelled from car windows or spewed by shocked pedestrians.

Society didn't want her to run very far. But when Merry ran far? She felt strong, pleasantly fatigued, energized. Sometimes a body knows what the judgmental minds around it do not.

She found another like-minded woman. Lyn. Married to an elite marathoner named Bob Carman, Lyn had the knowledge to teach Merry about pacing and training cycles and stretching. Merry and Lyn started running together with a group of men (coached by Bob) every day at five P.M. They all supported one another. These men understood what Lyn and Merry were capable of. Merry learned what it meant to become a serious long-distance runner.

And in 1963, if you were a serious long-distance runner, you almost inevitably wound up trying to run a marathon. More and more were cropping up around North America. So Merry and Lyn decided to take a shot—gender rules or no gender rules. Just before the starter's pistol fired at the Western Hemisphere Marathon—one of the top five marathons in America—the duo jumped from their hiding place and began to run behind the men.

Lyn dropped around mile twenty, leaving Merry to plug away for the final six miles alone. Taunts rained down from spectators. They asked her why she was doing this, told her to just give up already. She finished in 3:37:07. She beat five men. The race refused to acknowledge her as an official finisher, but a sympathetic official recorded her time. It was the first known female finish of a marathon since the distance was standardized at 26.2 miles. Before that, in 1926, a British runner named Violet Percy completed the London Marathon on a course measured at roughly twenty-one miles.

Between 1896 and 1963, it's likely that fewer than five women completed a race touted as a "marathon." In 1964, at least two others did: Dale Greig of the United Kingdom ran one in 3:27:45 and Mildred Sampson from New Zealand ran one in 3:19:33—the fastest known marathon time by a woman. In 1966, an American named Bobbi Gibb hid behind some bushes of her own before sneaking into and then completing the Boston Marathon.

By 1967—the year when Sy asked Maureen if she

wanted to run a marathon—it is likely fewer than ten women in the world were known to have done it in an official race. And among that list, there were no Canadian women. Millions and millions of others never got the chance. Secretly, many of them may have wanted to. But a powerful, poisonous word got to them first: *can't*.

They may have first heard it when they were toddlers, testing the speed of their tiny legs in the front yard, feeling like running was what they were born to do. *Girls can't run fast.* They may have heard it when they walked by a cinder track and watched boys glide by, running lap after lap. *Girls can't run long.* They may have heard it when they asked their parents to go to that track and see if they could do the same thing— run lap after lap. *Girls can't run with the boys.* They may have heard it when a local athletic organization put on a road race and they asked to join. *Girls can't run in races longer than 1.5 miles.*

Hear that word enough and it becomes ironclad fact. *Girls can't run marathons.*

It's not even worth trying.

With that barrage of *can'ts*, it's remarkable any women actually did try. They had to learn on their own that running was healthy and not harmful—even when the newspapers and strongmen and beauty experts said it wasn't. They had to find someone else who believed in them, who could teach them how to train and pace and hydrate. Sometimes, they had to find the perfect bushes to hide behind.

It's like trying to start a fire with flint and steel and no one there to teach you how. You have to get lucky—find the perfect tinder and kindling and arrange it in the perfect formation. Then you have to persevere, striking the flint and steel to create sparks and directing those sparks to that tinder, blowing on it just so to cause it to erupt into a flame. Then you have to tend to that flame, adding bigger and bigger sticks and then logs until it roars. Once it's big enough, you can share that fire. Others can come over and use it to light their own kindling.

Get enough fires going, and it's hard to put all the flames out.

***

If you're thirteen years old and you've run fifteen miles in one shot and you've never heard the names Pheidippides or Merry Lepper and your coach asks you to race most weekends, a marathon may not sound like that big of a deal.

Sy Mah, though, knew it was.

Sy loved when the girls he coached found success. He loved it when he saw Maureen in the backseat of the car on the way home from a race, curled up with a trophy. He loved standing along the course, throwing out encouragement and paces to will the girls to run faster. He wanted his athletes to be the very best they could. He wanted them to *never say die*.

When he watched Maureen nearly beat Roberta Picco at High Park under the yet-to-bloom cherry blossoms, he realized the very best for Maureen meant running longer. It meant the marathon.

In order to make that happen, though, he'd have to battle bureaucracy.

The AAU of Canada was founded on September 6, 1909. Like its counterpart in the United States, its mission was to develop and improve organized sport throughout the country. The organization built local offices to form teams and leagues around the country. They organized tournaments and championships in sports like hockey, baseball, and track and field. With the newly formed Olympics, Canada hoped to develop athletes who could compete on the international stage. The AAU hoped to be the organization to do it.

For the most part, it worked. Sports blossomed. It became easier and easier to find a team, practice, and compete in the game you loved, no matter where you lived.

But, like many official organizations around the

world at the time, the AAU didn't include everyone. From the early 1900s to the mid-twentieth century, the organization enforced racist rules that barred minorities and people of color from signing up for most sports.

The AAU also limited women to specific activities. They could play tennis or croquet—things accepted as fashionable and not too strenuous. They could run in AAU-sanctioned track-and-field meets, too, but only the shorter distances and only once they were a certain age.

The people in charge of the AAU enjoyed their power within sports. The position came with perks. When the Olympics came around, officials got a free overseas trip. There was prestige associated with a job at the AAU. Change threatened that prestige.

Lloyd Percival, the famous Canadian track coach of Olympian Abby Hoffman, saw the dangers of officials who coveted that prestige too much. He thought the AAU needed to change. He thought the organization had become too bloated, too powerful, and too mediocre. The AAU held athletes back from flourishing, from being their very best.

Sy Mah agreed.

But how do you change a slow-moving bureaucratic institution that likes its piles of paperwork and meetings and rules?

You might as well start by asking.

In the middle of April 1967, right after Maureen's breakout run against Roberta, Sy partnered with several local running clubs to organize the Eastern Canadian Centennial Marathon Championships, scheduled for May 6. In order for the race to happen, it needed approval from the AAU.

The race would have no problem getting it. The meet advisor, Dave Ellis, had peppered the local distance record books with unprecedented performances. It had an approved and measured course around York University, just a few miles from Earl Haig. It had enough volunteers to work as timers and pass out refreshments.

Sy wanted just one more thing: an official registration for Maureen.

As the race went through the approval process with the AAU, he put in a request to the organization to allow her to run. Newspapers perked up when they found out. On April 19, a local Toronto paper published the article "Mah vs. AAU Over Marathon."

The article quotes the national track-and-field chairman, Pete Beach, saying he was against it.

"If the girls run, then the AAU would be responsible for every other girl who entered," he said. "A few years ago, a girl would have been considered a freak to run long distances. Nobody's ever thought of it until lately."

He sent a clear message. *Girls can't run marathons.*

On the very same day newspaper printing presses stamped Pete Beach's words across a broadsheet—perhaps at the very same time Toronto residents read them over coffee and toast—another woman slipped on a pair of shoes in Boston, Massachusetts, to prove that wrong.

With that, another fire was about to start blazing.

15

In December 1966, months before Maureen had ever heard the word *marathon*, a twenty-year-old journalism student at Syracuse University decided she would run one.

Her name was Kathrine Switzer. And at the time she decided to run it, she was pissed.

That afternoon, a blizzard blew into her Upstate New York college town, blanketing the roads in four inches of snow. Kathrine slumped into her dormitory house, exhausted after a long day of classes, hoping to nap for a couple of hours before dinner. But a gregarious, balding mailman named Arnie Briggs wouldn't let her. He drove up in the storm and told her to get in the car. Despite the monstrous weather and rapidly setting sun, he wanted to go for a run.

Kathrine hemmed and hawed, but Arnie wouldn't leave. *Just a six-mile run. Easy!*

She proffered excuse after excuse. But after an hour of his pestering, she finally relented.

Arnie and Kathrine were an odd running pair. He was in his fifties — a World War II vet and devout

Catholic with a bum knee and a million stories that he loved to rattle off to anyone who would listen. She was a headstrong new student from Vienna, Virginia—long legged with wavy brown hair. And yet together they loped along the windy country roads and paths surrounding the university campus.

They'd met a few months earlier when Kathrine went out to the men's cross-country course to ask if she could run with the men's team. Arnie was the university mailman and former ranked marathoner who used to train with the team every afternoon, but now in his fifties, he acted as a kind of volunteer team manager. He was a kindly guy, and was happy to help anybody run, so when Kathrine showed up, he took her under his wing.

Her athletic career began in middle school, when Kathrine considered cheerleading. She didn't particularly like cheerleading, but it seemed like the popular thing to do—and a great way to get noticed by the captain of the football team.

Her father balked at the idea.

"The real game is on the field," he told her. "Life is for participating. Not spectating." That made sense to Kathrine. Why cheer for the action when she could be in it? So when she was twelve years old, she began running so she could hopefully make the school's field hockey team. Field hockey is like a cross between ice hockey and soccer. It's played on grass and with hockey sticks, with a soccer-sized field, a goal cage half the size of soccer's, and a small hard ball.

Choosing field hockey was a fortuitous decision. Out on the field, as she scrambled after the ball in a melee of girls her age, Kathrine discovered something new about herself: She was competitive. Other girls played because of the cute uniform skirts or because their parents made them. Kathrine wanted to *win*. And in order to win in field hockey, you have to run—long and fast.

Kathrine's mile-a-day training became the most important part of her day. It strengthened her and helped transform her into one of the best players on the field, someone who could outrun just about anyone else. Her training run also empowered her so much mentally that it gave her confidence in every aspect of her life.

By the time she finished high school, Kathrine was one of the best field hockey players in the area. But in the late 1960s, colleges didn't offer scholarships for women to play sports. At Syracuse, there weren't any women's intercollegiate sports at all. Which, Kathrine figured, was fine. As long as she didn't have to give up running, her greatest love. And that's how she met Arnie Briggs.

When she got to Syracuse University, she marched into the head coach's office of the men's cross-country team. She was a runner. Could she practice with the men?

The coach sent her out to ask Arnie, who was delighted she'd shown up. He wasn't quite fast enough to keep up with the gazellelike scholarship athletes (read: men) anymore, thanks to age and injuries. Kathrine wasn't quite fast enough to keep up with the men's team, either. But they could keep up with each other. Kathrine and Arnie made perfect running partners.

***

Unless it was snowing and dark and Kathrine had an empty stomach.

"Let me tell you about this one time at the Boston Marathon..." Arnie began. She groaned silently. She knew what was coming. Another classic Arnie story, one he'd repeated dozens of times on the many runs they'd completed together.

They were jogging an easy six miles from the school's field house and along Peck Hill Road—a familiar route for both of them. But by the halfway point, the snow was nearly six inches deep. It was bitter cold now, and they had to keep jumping out of the way of cars. The drivers probably couldn't see them on the hilly route through the gusting flakes. And worse: The dining halls were closing soon, which meant Kathrine would miss her opportunity for dinner.

All this was annoying, but she could deal with it. She could push through the final miles.

What she couldn't tolerate? *Another* story from Arnie Briggs about his precious Boston Marathon, the most prestigious marathon in the country. She'd heard about his fifteen finishes, the time he came in tenth place in excruciating heat, and so on and so on.

"Oh, Arnie, let's quit *talking* about the Boston Marathon and run the damn thing," she sniped.

Crabby and with snow up to her ankles, Kathrine had just suggested running a longer distance than she'd ever attempted. Much longer. And all because she was annoyed at Arnie.

"Oh, a *woman* can't run the Boston Marathon," he responded.

Arnie wasn't wrong about that. Women couldn't run the Boston Marathon because technically, according to the American AAU, women weren't legally allowed to compete in distances longer than 1.5 miles.

But Arnie wasn't citing the rule book. He was stating what he believed to be a fact of biology.

Once again, a female runner was hearing that word, *can't.* This time, from a trusted ally and training partner.

"With a marathon, it gets harder as it gets longer," he said. "Women can't do that kind of distance; they can't run that long."

On the shoulder of that road, in the raging blizzard, Kathrine grew angry. Furious. Determined.

She told Arnie he was wrong, that a woman named Bobbi Gibb had slipped out of the bushes and run the Boston Marathon that very year. Now it was Arnie's turn to get furious. "No dame ever ran no marathon!" he growled. He simply couldn't believe it. "I'd have to see it to believe it. And if you showed me in practice that you could do it, I'd even *take* you to the Boston Marathon!"

Instead of being discouraged, Kathrine was thrilled. He issued a challenge, and she saw a goal. She was going to prove to Arnie that she could do it.

***

There was no place to indicate if you were a man or a woman on the registration form for the 1967 Boston Marathon. And why would there be? It was just assumed that the hand filling out the simple white sheet of paper belonged to a man. After all, no woman had ever officially entered the oldest continually run marathon in the country.

Because this wasn't a race for women, at least according to the stuffy organization that put it on. The Boston Athletic Association was founded in 1887 as a club for wealthy Boston gentlemen to spend their leisure time playing sports. They built a clubhouse in the fashionable

Back Bay neighborhood of the city and filled it with a gymnasium, a bowling alley, billiards tables, and Turkish baths. They wore blazers and smoked cigars in the dining room after sweating on the state-of-the-art fitness equipment. In 1889, they acquired one of the city's first refrigerators to keep the food in their mahogany-paneled dining room fresh. They didn't allow women to be members.

The Boston Athletic Association founded the Boston Marathon in 1897 as a way to celebrate one of America's most historic and foundational moments: the Battles of Lexington and Concord, which kicked off the Revolutionary War in 1775. The race was held on April 19, which was the anniversary of those battles and also a statewide holiday in Massachusetts called Patriots' Day.

To the men who led the BAA, the reasons a woman shouldn't run this particular race were obvious. For one thing, women were simply not capable of running such a dangerously long distance—26 miles and 385 yards, starting in a sleepy town called Hopkinton, which is so far outside the city limits it can't even be considered a suburb.

But it wasn't just the length. The course is brutal. Sure, it feels easy for the first ten miles. The curvy two-lane road lulls you with gentle downhills and pretty views of church steeples and Victorian homes in New England towns that are older than America itself.

But then you hit the hills just outside Newton. Relentless, undulating menaces that over the decades have become the downfall of many would-be champions. One infamous section near mile twenty is literally called "Heartbreak Hill."

Because it was so hard, they knew for a fact that women's fragile bodies couldn't handle it.

It was obvious to the board members of the BAA why a woman shouldn't run the Boston Marathon. Why even bother putting it in the rule book?

In early 1967, when the registration form for a twenty-year-old member of the Syracuse Harriers running team arrived in the mail at the organization's headquarters on Boylston Street, it was processed with the rest. The name K. V. Switzer didn't cause any alarm. The men who organized the most famous marathon in the world didn't mark it as different or special. They put it in the pile with the hundreds of others. In a few weeks, the men who filled out those sheets of paper would arrive for the seventieth edition of the race.

And so would a woman.

***

Kathrine had already run more than twenty-six miles in one shot by the time she hopped in a car to drive the three hundred miles east to Boston with Arnie and her boyfriend, Tom. After their run in the blizzard, Arnie—skeptical at first—became excited at the prospect of helping Kathrine run the race he loved so much. But in order to be sure she could do it, he wanted to do a trial run first. So they built up their mileage during the first months of 1967, then a few weeks before the actual race they headed out to try to finish 26.2 miles. By the end, Kathrine still felt great—albeit with some nasty blisters on her feet—and she suggested they run another five miles "just to be sure of the distance." Arnie, on the other hand, was staggering. She had to support his arm in the last mile of their now-legendary 31-mile run.

She, quite nearly, had run a marathon veteran into the ground. She was ready.

She wasn't so sure about her boyfriend, Tom, though. He was a hulking and handsome track coach at Syracuse who specialized in throwing shot-put, discus, and hammer. At the last moment, he'd decided to tag along—on little training—to prove that he, too, could finish the race.

On Patriots' Day that year, 733 runners huddled in the starting corral on Main Street in the middle of Hopkinton. Despite wearing a bulky sweatshirt to ward off the freezing cold and trying to keep a low profile, Kathrine noticed that the men jostling and stretching around her seemed pleased—if a little surprised—that a woman was in their midst. One asked if he could take a picture with her, another for tips for getting his wife to start running. They were welcoming.

She was jittery at the start like all marathoners, but she didn't have the pressure of being the first— that honor had come the year before, when Bobbi Gibb, then Bobbi Bingay, hid in the bushes with a hood pulled over her head before sneaking onto the course. Kathrine didn't need to hide and warmed up on side streets along with the men. And she was an official entrant— Arnie had insisted that she officially register and pay her two-dollar entry fee. "You're a member of the AAU and you must follow the rules," he said.

What Kathrine didn't know as she loped down Route 135 in the first mile of the race was that Bobbi was nearby—having jumped onto the course from the bushes to tackle the race for the second time.

But while Bobbi remained incognito without a race bib (her race entry the previous year had been rejected by the BAA), Kathrine stood out. A white bib with black block lettering that read "261" fluttered across the front of her chest and on her back. It meant she was an official entrant, and the men running around her were encouraging and motivating.

Once she started running, Kathrine settled into a rhythm, letting the first few miles slip by as she, Arnie, and Tom chatted. Things seemed calm.

That is, until a truck loaded with press photographers followed by a bus carrying race officials lumbered by on the left. The journalists were shocked to see a woman with an official bib on the course. They fumbled to get their cameras in position to snag a photo.

But who was even more shocked than the photographers to see a woman on the course wearing an official bib? The codirector of the race, Jock Semple.

While the cameras clicked away, Jock—his face seething—sprinted behind Kathrine. He clawed at the bib numbers pinned to the front and back of her shirt, but failed to rip them off.

"Get the hell out of my race and give me those numbers!" he raged.

Tom, much bigger and stronger than Semple, grabbed the official and violently shoved him to the side. Kathrine was dazed but kept running.

The entire scene was captured by the photographers on the truck. They now had a breaking story on their hands. A woman, with official numbers, was on her way to finish the race—and finish despite the organizer of that race trying to force her off the course.

The journalists zoomed away to start working on the story.

Kathrine kept running. She now had even more reason to finish. She needed to prove to Jock Semple and all the angry men like him that she belonged. She settled back into her stride, determined to make it to the end.

A few hours later, she did. To little fanfare. Most of the spectators had packed up and gone home by the time she reached Boylston Street.

Freezing cold and wet like everyone else, she jumped in the car with Tom and Arnie to head home. As they drove on the interstate, a series of journalists pecked furiously at their typewriters. They were on deadline. They needed to file breaking news: A woman with an official bib had completed the most famous marathon in the world for the first time.

One of those journalists would give his copy to an editor. That editor would send it to press. That press would stamp the news in ink on a broadsheet paper. And that paper would be delivered to the suburban homes in North York, Canada, where a running coach was ardently training his own female athlete to run a marathon.

When Sy Mah heard the news about Kathrine Switzer, he got an idea about how he might add even more drama to Maureen's marathon effort.

16

Maureen didn't have much time to get ready for her first marathon. "Do you want another girl to run the race with you?" Sy asked Maureen as he approached her on Earl Haig's cinder track. She'd just completed a workout. They'd been getting longer, and at a slower pace, than she was used to. He had changed her training in preparation for the 26.2 miles she'd be completing in a few short weeks.

"Sure," Maureen responded. "That would be great!"

It didn't seem like that big of a deal, that question. Just another scheme by Coach. If he thought it would help to have another girl in the race, that was fine by Maureen. The more the merrier, she thought. But to her, it didn't really make a difference if another runner joined the race—girl or boy. She knew, deep in her powerful heart and leg muscles, that she could finish. She'd built up to running eighteen miles in a single workout. She felt strong, and so far the distance in training felt easy.

She walked over to her bike. Sy neglected to tell her who, precisely, the "girl" was who would be joining her at the starting line. He also didn't tell her that she had already finished a marathon. Maureen didn't care to ask. She rode home on her bike.

***

The phone in the front entryway of the old three-story wooden house where Kathrine lived wouldn't stop ringing. Journalists from around the country dialed the ramshackle house on Comstock Avenue on the Syracuse University campus. They wanted to speak to the rebel, the woman who'd defied the Boston Athletic Association. The *New York Times* called. So did the Associated Press. Eventually, the *Tonight Show* with Johnny Carson—one of the most widely watched evening programs in America—made it through. Everyone wanted Kathrine's story.

"Hello? Who is this?" Kathrine asked into the receiver. She expected it to be another journalist.

"Hi. This is S—." The end of the name got muddled. It was a man's voice. He spoke quickly. He sounded excited.

"I'm sorry, who? Can you repeat your name?" Kathrine asked.

The man did, spewing out the syllables in rapid succession. She still couldn't hear it. Something with an *S* and an *M*. It sounded to her like he said "Silas Marner."

But that couldn't be. That was the name of a book from the 1860s she'd studied in her English literature class.

The man enunciated so she could hear more clearly through the wires.

"My name is Sy Mah. I am calling from Canada. I coach the North York Track Club."

Kathrine wasn't sure how this man got her number. But her interest was piqued when she heard the word *Canada*. She loved going across the border. As a kid, she always thought the Canadian side of Niagara Falls was a lot more beautiful than the American side. Every now and then she and Tom went on day road trips from Syracuse to the border, which was only a few hours' drive.

Sy didn't want to hear Kathrine's story. He'd already read all about it. Instead, he had an invitation.

"We're hosting a marathon over here in Toronto on May sixth. Do you want to come run it?"

The question surprised Kathrine. In that moment, she expected never to be allowed to run in another marathon (or even an official race) again. The American AAU had sent her a letter stating as much.

The envelope Kathrine received from the AAU had displayed a "special delivery" stamp in the corner, meaning someone had spent a fortune to rush it to her mailbox. It came just two days after she'd returned home—so fast that someone had to have put it in the mail the same day she ran the Boston Marathon.

The letter notified Kathrine, Tom, and her coach, Arnie, that they'd all been expelled from the American AAU. They'd no longer be welcome at any of the association's sanctioned races—essentially all the races in the country.

Kathrine fumed. She burned her membership card. She wanted nothing to do with race organizers.

Until Canada came calling.

Sy promised to cover gas money if Kathrine, Tom, and Arnie decided to drive the five hours east around Lake Ontario—not a small expense.

Kathrine gladly agreed. She felt as if she was getting away with mischief—like she was sticking her tongue out at the American AAU. If they didn't want her to run in the States? Fine. She'd just go to Canada.

**

But Canada wasn't so keen on having her come, either.

As Maureen trained around the quiet streets of North York and Kathrine resumed her undergraduate studies at the Newhouse School at Syracuse University, Sy attended meetings with the Canadian AAU. South of the border, the American wing of the organization had made their position clear: If a woman chose to run a marathon, she'd be blacklisted. Sy hoped the Canadian counterparts would be more lenient.

In some ways they were. At a final meeting, held in the third week of April, officials cleared the way for women to run in Sy's marathon. But their approval came with a caveat—a big one. The Canadian AAU wouldn't recognize Maureen and Kathrine as official entrants. They could run the distance, they could expend the same amount of sweat and energy as the men, but their effort wouldn't count. Because to make the run official meant writing Maureen's and Kathrine's names in an official program. It meant marking their times down on a piece of paper once they finished. It meant sending that sheet of paper to the AAU so they could record the results and review them for records. It meant acknowledging that they'd been wrong for decades. It meant finally agreeing that women could run marathons. The officials at the AAU didn't want any of that. They wanted, on paper at least, for Maureen and Kathrine's marathon to not exist.

It's a similar story that had been repeated a small handful of times around the world, from Melpomene in Greece to Merry Lepper in California to Mildred Sampson in New Zealand. A woman would run the full distance, then the authorities would say it didn't count because of the rules—rules, of course, which they had made.

The only way word spread that these women had finished a marathon? Through newspapers. But even then, in a printed publication, the feats came with an asterisk. The world "unofficial" almost always preceded the reporting of the result. Mildred Sampson, for example, was always introduced on the page as the "unofficial" world record holder in the marathon with her time of three hours and nineteen minutes. At the very least, Sy figured, the papers acknowledged the accomplishment. The more they acknowledged it, he thought, the more other girls might see it and know that a marathon was possible. Sy just needed to make sure the papers would come.

On a beige sheet of paper under a pink North York Track Club header, Sy used a typewriter to make sure they did. He wrote a letter to Kathrine.

"I know the AAU is not anxious to have me publicize the unofficial ladies' entries," he wrote. "However, when you are certain that you can come I hope that you will allow us to mention it to the press. The purpose is not sensationalism; I feel that we must break down these silly notions that still exist that women cannot run long distances and your entry in this easy field should put that message across very well."

Mah wanted that message to ring loud and clear. He'd been putting the pieces together to make sure the world knew Maureen and Kathrine's marathon *would* exist. In order to do that, though, he needed something big to happen. He needed the papers to cover the event. He needed some kindling.

Back when he'd first approached Maureen and asked her if she wanted to run the race, he followed up with a second question.

"Do you want to break a world record?"

"Sure!" she responded.

***

Kathrine, Arnie, Tom, and another member of the Syracuse Harriers running club pulled into the quiet streets of North York, Ontario, late in the evening on May 5, 1967. On the car ride up, they chatted about the race. They were excited for the opportunity to run a marathon again, but they were also wary of this little thirteen-year-old girl they heard would be running it.

After suffering through the pain of running a marathon—injuries common to all long-distance runners include chafed thighs and nipples, bruised toenails, blistered feet—Kathrine worried that the marathon was too far for any kid, boy or girl, to run.

She hadn't met Maureen yet, but something felt off to her. Was this Sy Mah coach exploiting this girl? Were her parents pushing her too hard?

Sy greeted the New York caravan on a sidewalk near his home. Kathrine noticed he was short, skinny, and wore a funny hat and glasses. His body appeared to thrum with as much energy as his rapid-fire talk. He didn't seem like a huckster or some greasy politician, hoping to amass fame and fortune off his very young star athlete.

To Kathrine, he looked more—well—like a geek.

Most men interested in long-distance running then did seem like geeks. They ran with short running shorts hiked up around their waist with a cotton T-shirt or singlet tucked into the elastic band. They were different. Weird, even. But passionate enough about long-distance running that they welcomed others into the experience—like Kathrine and Maureen. The sport coats in charge just didn't seem to understand the invitation.

Sy looked to Kathrine like the many long-distance runners she'd met. She liked him.

"Where's a good place to get dinner around here?" she asked. She was starving.

"It's pretty late, so most places are closed," he responded. Then he smiled. "But don't worry, there's always Chinese."

This option very much worried Kathrine. She wasn't used to eating Chinese food, and she didn't want to eat something that might upset her stomach the night before a race. But she had no other choice.

Kathrine ordered fried shrimp and rice. She ate it knowing that tomorrow she wouldn't have to sneak around a starting corral and hide that she was a woman. The weather was supposed to be nice. She planned on wearing matching maroon shorts and a top—the same outfit she had worn at Boston under her sweats.

The meal tasted fantastic.

***

Maureen's dinner came with a side of nerves.

Not about the race itself. She felt ready for the speed and the distance. She was nervous about everything else.

The past few days, it had felt like there was a string tied around her waist pulling tighter and tighter. She'd seen the newspaper clipping that detailed Sy's fight with the AAU. He had told her mom to keep quiet about the record attempt. After practices, the adults in the club seemed more on edge than usual.

But the absolute worst part about the lead-up to the race came Friday evening, when Margaret took Maureen to the doctor. Maureen *hated* doctors. Ever since she was a toddler, the clean, sterile offices and old men with metal stethoscopes terrified her. But her mom insisted. This was Sy's plan. He needed a note proving she was healthy enough to run the race. But more important, Sy predicted people would question more than just Maureen's ability. He wanted a medical professional to provide written proof that Maureen was a girl.

At thirteen, Maureen didn't understand the implications. She sat inside the office, just nervous to be around the scary-looking medical tools and charts. The doctor she'd been seeing for years walked into the room. He took her pulse and asked her a few questions. He filled out some information on a clipboard and sent her home.

Tension had been building, and she could feel it tied directly to her.

That night before the race, her thoughts swirled. What if she didn't belong? What if she wasn't supposed to be there? There was a conflict and she was at the center of it. She knew that there were people who didn't want her to run.

17

Maureen looked small standing in the grass on the side of the cracked asphalt road, like a loitering kid who'd snuck into an event for adults. Newspapers regularly commented on her size when they reported on her races around Canada and the United States. They called her "little" and "tiny." She was—even at thirteen—still a petite four foot eight and eighty pounds. But if size is just a comparison from one thing to another, then what the reporters observed when Maureen raced against girls and boys nearly her own age was nothing compared to the whir of activity around her now.

Here on Steeles Avenue, just north of the new brick buildings at York University, ten minutes from home, Maureen had never looked smaller.

Twenty-eight grown men stretched and jogged and chatted along the road. They looked like billowing trees in a storm. Maureen stood at the edge of the motion, reluctant to enter the fray.

"You have to go now," Margaret pleaded firmly to her daughter. "The race is about to start."

Nerves burbled in Maureen's stomach. Not for the race—the race she could handle. But for the idea of approaching these men. She knew some of them; they ran with Sy on weeknights at the track. The ones she didn't know looked friendly enough in their cotton T-shirts and scrunched-down socks. But she worried what they would think when she approached, in her maroon shorts and singlet—a uniform that all but announced her intention to run with them.

What will they say? Maureen wondered.

"You need to go. Now," her mom said. "They are about to start."

Maureen pulled off her baggy sweatpants—the same ones she hated people to see—and trudged toward the crowd of runners. As the men continued to stretch and jostle and crack jokes, their lanky limbs whirled as if caught by a gust of wind peeling down the road. They were warmed up.

As she shuffled closer to them, Maureen felt like she'd entered a restricted room during an important meeting. Like when you accidentally open the wrong door and everyone turns their head toward you and the whole space falls dead silent. She walked right next to the men, the top of her brown hair barely reaching their torsos. They parted ways to let her through. Some of them looked confused.

Maybe this girl is mistaken? Shouldn't she be with the other girls?

The other girls were off to the side. There were a few dozen of them, waiting for their own race—a five-mile women's open that would start once the main event kicked off. The main event: the marathon.

Only one other female approached the starting line—Kathrine. But Maureen didn't even notice. She was wrapped up in her own thoughts and fears. She worried what everyone might think. Not just the people here, but people everywhere. She felt so small. Little.

"Runners, take your mark," a man yelled from the side of the road.

Sy approached and took his spot next to Maureen. He was racing as well. He wore shorts and a T-shirt, his usual black glasses perched on his nose.

"Get set."

The group took a collective breath. Maureen's muscles clenched. She looked straight ahead. To the left, she could see the cluster of brick buildings. To the right, unkempt grass and farmland. The road wasn't closed, but even at 11:59 A.M. on a Saturday, there were no cars. The men dissolved in her peripheral vision. This felt familiar—the quiet tension in the moments before the pistol fires.

Crack!

Twenty-eight men, a young woman from Syracuse University, and a thirteen-year-old girl from just up the road began to amble west.

Only one of them was trying to break a world record.

***

This pace is soooooo slow, Maureen thought after the first mile. The easy effort felt like a warm-up.

She settled into a running rhythm near a group of men at the middle of the pack. Sy ran next to her. He expected to stay by her side through the whole race, helping her keep on track. This was Maureen's first marathon. But it was Sy's first marathon, too. He also was confident he could keep up because, one mile in, this speed felt easy to him, too.

Seven minutes and thirty seconds. She needed to hit this pace perfectly at each mile marker. Like a metronome.

That's a fast clip for a beginner. But Maureen felt, gliding on muscular legs that had completed thousands of miles in training, like she could do this forever.

It was a strange feeling for her. In typical races, the tension doesn't cease after the starting gun goes off. Your legs fire off the line. You can't relax, your muscles burn. You begin to breathe hard. You can't speak or smile or wave.

Maureen was doing all three in the first miles. She'd never felt so wistful and at ease during a competition before. She was just happy to be away from the starting line, away from the tension. She was doing what she loved to do. She was running. Albeit running really, really slowly. For her, that is.

Seven minutes and thirty seconds. Seven minutes and thirty seconds.

That's what she kept thinking, repeating the time in her mind as she jaunted through the first mile, then the second, then the third, like clockwork. Except Maureen didn't need a clock. She didn't need someone at each mile marker to tell her how fast her pace was. She could feel it, within a few steps one way or the other.

In practice, Sy could tell her to run 400 meters in seventy-five seconds. She usually missed that time by less than a second. She knew that with the smallest adjustment in how hard her foot struck the ground or how quickly the breath sucked into her lungs and blew out her nose, she could change her pace.

Mile four: seven minutes and thirty seconds.
Mile five: seven minutes and thirty seconds.

This was easy. It was fun. Maureen was next to her

coach on a deserted two-lane road just a short distance from her house. It was a weekend day in May and she was going to the cottage soon.

"Gee," she said to the crowd standing near the refreshment stand at the end of the first lap. "This is great!"

**

There's really only one word that can accurately describe the course of the Eastern Canadian Centennial Marathon Championships.

Boring.

It was selected for its remoteness. In 1967, you couldn't just close down miles and miles of busy road for only thirty people to have a footrace, so you had to go to where the cars weren't. At noon on a weekend in May, that happened to be around York University. The campus sat on a parcel of wispy grass surrounded by farmland northwest of downtown Toronto.

The route consisted of five laps, each just over five miles long. Each lap followed four two-lane roads, forming a box that framed the college. Runners hoping for a distraction from the repetitive running drudgery would only get roughly the same view—brick buildings to the left and a green, brown, and beige expanse of flat fields to the right. It was the type of scenery you'd forget about during a long road trip. For hours, they would literally be running in rectangular loops.

Maureen didn't mind in the least bit.

This was, to her, a weekend gathering of her best friends and their parents. The scenery didn't matter because the people she was with helped the miles glide by. There was Sy, ready to offer a joke or quick word of encouragement or update on the pace. Each time she ran north on Keele Street up a gentle hill before the final left turn of the lap, she knew she was about to cross through a mini cheering section, filled with all the people who'd supported her the past three years. The people who let her run.

There was Mr. Sim, who instead of waiting with his motorcycle to take her to Dairy Queen was in charge of controlling traffic—what little there was. There was his wife, Joan, plus Sy's daughters, Brenda and Bonnie, standing behind a little table with a fluttering sign taped to the front that read REFRESHMENT STAND. They handed her paper cups filled with water and a sugary orange-flavored drink each lap. The chief course marshal, in charge of watching over the race to make sure everyone ran the full distance, was John Dovaston—father of one of her friends in the club, Steve. Maureen's dad, Roger, and Jo-Ann's dad, Joe, stood at corners of the route, also acting as course marshals.

Her mom, Margaret, had taken the day off from work to watch the race. She wouldn't have to rush to the phone at Eaton's to find out how her daughter finished.

The nervousness from the start line had completely melted away as Maureen ticked off a second and third lap. This felt less like a race and more like everything she had come to love about running—the satisfying, repetitive bounce of moving forward, surrounded by the people she cared about most.

Seven minutes and thirty seconds.

Seven minutes and thirty seconds.

The pressure peeled away like an onion. This felt like no race she'd ever run before. There weren't any girls to chase after, except the one she didn't know (Kathrine fell far behind Maureen from the start). No Roberta Picco to try to out-sprint. No burning, aching lungs, desperately trying to motor her to a finish line.

At the end of each lap, she stopped and crouched behind a canvas tent staked into the ground. It served as a little bathroom for runners. Maureen thought this was funny, that in the middle of a race, when nature came knocking, she had time to pee and was still hitting her goal pace each mile.

The distance floated by with cheers from friends and parents. This felt so easy, Maureen began to wonder what the big deal was. Why did she have to feel so uncomfortable at the start line of this race? Why did she have to feel like she didn't belong? Why did anyone want to stop her from running a marathon when it felt this effortless and this fun?

Seven minutes and thirty seconds.

Complete a few more miles, and Maureen Wilton would be the first woman in Canada to finish a marathon. Continue at the current pace, and she'd be the fastest woman in the world to ever do it. History is funny. Those who make it often don't know they're making it in the moment. Maureen certainly didn't.

***

But here's the thing about marathons. They *aren't* easy. They exist because of a battle, a battle fought thousands of years ago, and in some ways, that's exactly what they are. You fight with your body, asking it to do probably more than it has ever done before. Often, it fights back.

Sy didn't want to show it, but this run was hurting him more than any other run he'd done in his life. His muscles ached. His feet had several painful hot spots.

He'd run with Maureen for fifteen miles. He wasn't sure how much longer he could last.

"I have to hit the head," he told her. "Keep going. I'll catch up."

She smiled and floated away.

How could this look so easy for her?

He knew the answer, of course. Under his guidance, she'd been training for three years. Her body was primed to devour this kind of distance. She'd put in hard work so that this would feel effortless.

When he ducked into the canvas tent, he knew he wouldn't ever catch up. He emerged and Maureen was gone. His muscles were seizing and he started to move like the Tin Man from *The Wizard of Oz* without the oil, jerking forward in an unnatural shuffle. At mile twenty, having no idea where Maureen was, he slumped to the curb.

Why do all these people have to be here? he thought. *I don't want to run anymore. I can't make another lap. It would kill me.*

He pulled off his left shoe. The cotton sock was soaking from both sweat and a clear viscous goop. A massive blister had formed on the sole of his foot and popped a few miles back. Now he had a flaming red patch of skin that seared every time he took a step.

His motto may have been "Never say die," yet here

he was, splayed on the side of the road saying "die" and grappling with the fact that, until this moment, he truly didn't understand what a marathon was. He had never run this far before in his life.

Sure, he knew the basics of it—the stuff anyone can find out if they read the papers or running magazines that Sy devotedly subscribed to. He knew that because it is so long and so tremendously difficult, there is honor in simply finishing, no matter how fast. In 1967, not many people in the world had done it.

That appealed to Sy. He didn't consider himself a fast runner; he called himself a "duffer," an idiot new-comer. He felt incompetent. Sometimes when he was with his friends, the adult men who ran and won local races around southern Canada, Sy felt like he didn't belong.

But sitting on the side of the road with one more lap to go in the hardest run of his life, Sy wasn't faring much worse than most of those other men—however experienced they were. A few had already called it quits. The refreshment stand and a seat in the grass were just too tempting compared to the thought of continuing another lap, alone.

Jo-Ann, spectating on a remote corner of the route, watched a forty-five-year-old runner she didn't know

collapse into a ditch on the side of the road, screaming in agony. She suspected he was suffering muscle
cramps.

Maureen started noticing the carnage, too. After lap
one, her metronomelike pace never wavering, she came
through near the refreshment stand in sixteenth place.
By the end of lap two, she'd moved into fourteenth. The
field of runners had stretched out enough that most ran
alone or in small groups of two or three. The ambitious
runners at the start began slowing down in the third
lap, their bodies giving them a hard lesson in reality.

When Maureen came through the starting area for
the fourth lap, her teammates hopped onto the street
and ran with her to keep her company. They passed
four more men over the next five miles. Coming into
the final lap, Maureen had moved up to eighth place.
Somewhere behind her, the men who were allowed to
run this race because of their strong bodies and masculine minds hobbled forward. The girl who wasn't supposed to be able to do this smiled to her friends and
waved. She only had one five-mile lap to go.

***

Margaret Wilton squinted at the face of her mechanical Bulova watch. It had blue stones encrusted around

a stretchy band. The hands twitched across the watch face, as if they were just as nervous as Margaret.

Maureen's running late, she thought to herself. She squinted south down Keele Street, then back at her watch. She was worried. She'd camped herself on the curb, just before the final left turn—precisely a mile from the finish line.

Sure, it would be amazing to watch her daughter lean breathlessly past the timekeeper to claim a world's best time, but Margaret felt like she had a job to do. She wanted to be the one to tell Maureen her final pace, to break the news—good or bad—on whether a world's best time would be possible. She'd be a comforting face in the closing stage of the longest run of Maureen's life. Because that's what moms are for. Not to watch the finish from the side of the road. But to help when it matters most.

Five men passed Margaret in different states of despair. The leader, Jim Beisty, looked pained yet determined. Minutes behind him, a college-aged kid named Jim Rea streaked by, looking stronger than anyone should after twenty-five miles of running. The others looked like zombies. You couldn't say they were running a marathon as much as shuffling through it.

But where was Maureen? What would she look like?

The race had started at noon. Maureen needed to cross the finish line by 3:19 P.M. She needed to reach Margaret by 3:11 P.M.

The tiny hands on the watch's face crept ahead.

***

Seven minutes and thirty seconds. Mile twenty-one.

Seven minutes and thirty seconds. Mile twenty-two.

Maureen didn't wear a watch, but she could feel herself locked in on the pace. It never crossed her mind that she could be off. Course marshals and teammates and parents frequently yelled out the time. She'd been right on the nose at mile twenty, and it felt like she hadn't slowed since.

Around mile twenty-five, running north on Keele Street, up a little hill, Maureen saw her mom. Margaret checked her watch again. Then looked up furtively.

"You're too slow, you're not going to make it!" Margaret yelled as Maureen hustled by.

The news hit Maureen like a slap. She turned her head, midstride. "What do you mean I am too slow?" she yelled, already too far away to hear a response. She was frustrated. Annoyed.

She didn't understand. She thought she'd hit each and every mile at the right pace.

A little voice inside her head punctured her thoughts. *Maybe you were wrong? Maybe you were too slow?*

The twenty-fifth mile of a marathon is a disorienting place. Willpower tends to fade and you're a lot more likely to heed the temptation of that little voice. It'll ask you to ease off, slow down. Take a breather. Why bother when you can't beat the time you wanted anyway?

Unless you're fiercely competitive. Then you ignore the voice and try anyway.

Maureen changed gears. She accelerated like you would in a sports car on an empty freeway. If she was gliding before, now she flew. Faster and faster her legs churned, up to a six-minute-per-mile pace. If she wasn't going to break a world's best time, she could at least prove she was capable of finishing a marathon.

She took a left on Steeles Avenue. She could see the little white poster on the wood stake that read MARA-THON FINISH. Her hair whipped higher as her elbows punched the air by her neck. She sprinted. Her brother Gord, who had been standing on the side of the road with a quarter mile to go, jumped in beside her, keeping by her side, stride for stride, willing her forward.

As she bolted to the finish line, Maureen didn't know two things. First, whether she had run fast enough to break Mildred Sampson's mark of three hours and nineteen minutes. Second, that no Canadian woman before her had ever completed a marathon.

She knew only one thing. There was a finish line a few feet away, and she was going to burst across it using every ounce of energy she had left. She careened forward then slowed to a stop. She took deep breaths.

"Did she break the record?" someone yelled.

"Do we even know if she ran the whole way?"

PART III

THE RECORD

18

An eerie mist blanketed National Stadium in Tokyo, Japan, on the afternoon of October 21, 1964. In the thick, soupy air, sixty-eight men from thirty-five countries jiggled their shoulders and legs behind a white chalk line on a cinder track. As the pistol fired, the seventy-five thousand people crammed in the bowl-shaped concrete-and-steel structure erupted. The men glided around the track nearly two times before exiting through a tunnel out to a paved street in the heart of the city. Behind stanchions and ropes, thousands more spectators in rows three to four deep screamed as the horde ran by. The Olympic Marathon was under way, and the globe watched with bated breath.

A man wearing a green singlet and maroon shorts eased into the mass of runners from the back. If you were able to watch the first three or so miles of the race, you may not have even noticed him. He was in sixth place. Yet every metronomic stride he took had just a bit more power than that of those around him. He gained on the leaders inch by inch, footstep by footstep, until he passed them all. By the halfway point, he led by two seconds. By the twenty-sixth mile, he led by more than four minutes—an eternity. Far behind, men staggered to the side of the road. They bent to their knees and poured cool water over their heads. Ten of them quit.

From a distance, the man in the green singlet looked skinny—even frail. But the closer he came, the clearer you could see the contours of his chiseled muscles. He looked like he was meant to run the way a plane looks like it is meant to fly. His name was Abebe Bikila, and he made the marathon look easy.

Born in a mountainous region of Ethiopia in 1932, Bikila was athletically gifted from a young age. When he grew up, he moved to Addis Ababa, the nation's capital, and enlisted as a member of the Imperial Palace Bodyguard. It was there, while serving, that he spotted a group of men in gorgeous uniforms. A little fire of longing sparked inside him. He *wanted* one of those uniforms.

Bikila learned that the group of men had earned the clothing by representing Ethiopia at the 1956 Melbourne Olympics. They were athletes. If competing in the Olympics was what it took to dress like those men, Bikila decided he would get there. Long-distance running, he discovered, was his best chance to do so. By 1960, he'd trained hard enough to qualify for the marathon at the games in Rome. His racing shoes fell apart on the journey over and the new pair he tested from an Italian store caused horrible blisters. So he ran the race barefoot. And still won. Four years later, he returned, showing the same natural talent—the same beautiful running ease—as before. The only difference? He wore a pair of gleaming white Puma sneakers.

As Bikila reentered Tokyo's National Stadium, completely alone, waves of applause crashed down upon him. His singlet was saturated with so much sweat and water, it appeared nearly black. But his form showed almost no sign of fatigue. He broke a thin string at the finish line, inspiring radio announcers to bellow amazed commentary into microphones. Television cameras rolled as he promptly began doing stretches and calisthenics on the grassy infield. A scoreboard flashed his time for the enormous crowd to see. Two hours, twelve minutes, 11.2 seconds.

Abebe Bikila had just smashed the marathon world record, making him one of the most famous athletes on the planet.

Across his chest in black lettering over a white background, he wore bib number 17.

***

Maureen didn't notice the smattering of applause from the few dozen people standing on the edge of the desolate road as she braked to a stop next to the hand-written finish line sign posted in the grass. Her head buzzed with thoughts, almost as fast as her heart raced.

Did I do it? Did I break the record?

She walked toward the group of North York Track Club girls standing near the curb.

"Great job," one of them said.

"Incredible," another added. Maureen couldn't tell who said what, still lost in her doubts and frustration.

What do they mean by "good job"? I didn't even get the result I was supposed to.

There was no big scoreboard to display her time as she crossed the line, and Maureen simply refused to run with a bulky stopwatch—the only way you could keep accurate time on a run in 1967. She had no idea how she'd finished. She just knew, because her mom said so, that she'd been too slow.

This wasn't how she was supposed to feel at the end of the race. Like she had let everyone down. *It would be different if the pace hadn't been so easy for twenty-five miles*, Maureen thought. Maybe if Sy had let her run harder, if she could have felt the satisfying zip and pain in her speedy legs a little earlier, this failure wouldn't sting so much. Twenty-six point two miles is an awfully long way to run and fail, especially in front of your closest friends and family.

The paper bib pinned to her chest crinkled as she dejectedly walked closer to her teammates. It displayed the number 17.

***

A mechanical watch is like a long-distance runner's body. It's composed of hundreds of minuscule parts that all must work together harmoniously to keep everything moving forward at the right pace. If a paper-thin spring goes out of alignment, if lubrication between the gears wears thin, the hands can move forward a fraction of a second too slow or too fast. That adds up over hours or days or months, which means a beloved Bulova watch with blue gems around a stretchy band can end up showing the completely wrong time.

Margaret Wilton had relied on that watch, and she had yelled out the incorrect time to her daughter.

Maureen hadn't just broken the world's fastest marathon time. She'd smashed it.

"You did it!" Sheila yelled at Maureen, smiling. "You actually did it."

"What do you mean I did it?" Maureen responded. "I didn't do it. My mom said I was too slow."

"She's wrong. She's really wrong. You broke the record!"

Frustration morphed into confusion in Maureen's

head. Then came relief. That's why her teammates looked so happy. She suddenly heard the clapping from the people standing around her. She noticed the smiles. She hadn't failed after all.

"So what was my time?" she asked.

Before she heard the answer, a tall man Maureen didn't recognize trudged over to the group of girls. He carried a clipboard and wore long dress pants and a sweater. He was not a parent or a member of the North York Track Club. Maureen guessed he was a course marshal—someone hired to monitor the race—or a member of the Canadian AAU.

"Did you run that whole way, miss?" the man asked sternly. He looked down at her like a teacher would, asking a student if they'd been passing notes.

A small pang of confusion hit Maureen's chest.

Then that pang turned to anger. She couldn't believe what this man was asking. No, not just asking. *Accusing.* He thought she cheated.

Maureen had been training for three years. She'd completed thousands of miles around the dusty cinder track at Earl Haig, on the smooth and punishingly hard cement inside the North York Centennial Arena, through a cemetery, in front of a mayor in Baltimore, and among the nearly bloomed cherry blossoms in

High Park. She'd been awarded medals and trophies and shiny blue ribbons from the most competitive youth women's running events in North America. *Of course* she'd run the whole race.

From a distance, though, you might think Maureen looked skinny and little—frail even. It wasn't until you got closer and you could see the sharp contours of her chiseled muscles that you'd realize she looked like she was meant to run the same way a plane looks like it is meant to fly.

She stared the man straight in the eye. Panic and frustration soured inside her stomach. She felt like she was in trouble. But for what? All she did was run a race. There were people with her almost the entire way! This man, standing more than a head above her, made her feel, once again, like she shouldn't be there.

"Yes, sir. I did," she said meekly.

In three hours, fifteen minutes, and 22.8 seconds. Sixth place overall and ahead of twenty-three men (seven of whom quit) and Kathrine. Faster than any woman had ever completed the distance. Not just in Toronto or in Canada or even in North America. Maureen was the fastest female marathon runner in the world.

***

An hour or so after he had the fastest men's marathon time in the world, Abebe Bikila stood atop a tiered podium, rising a head taller than everyone else in the infield. More than seventy-five thousand people watched the flag of his country rise and flutter on a pole—the Olympic flame glowing in the background. Bikila was presented with a gold medal. A few days later, the Ethiopian government awarded him a car.

Twenty minutes or so after Maureen Wilton accomplished the same exact feat, she stood by the finish line, waiting for her struggling coach. A doctor had come by to check her pulse. He found it to be normal. The other parents must have convinced the stern official that she'd finished the whole race, because he didn't pester her again. But Maureen couldn't shake the accusation. She didn't feel happy or accomplished. She worried about what the adults were saying. There was no medal ceremony. No podium. But word began to spread about her accomplishment.

Gord Sim jumped on his motorcycle and rumbled down the road to find Sy. The coach did not look good. Rather than running, he was moving forward in a painful shuffle, wincing with every step.

"Moe made it in three-fifteen," Gord said ecstatically.

"Holy smokes, she's broken the record," Sy said. "This will go all around the world!" At the final aid station, he slugged down an entire cup of tea with honey. The news of Moe and the drink helped him stumble on with slightly more strength.

"I can't wait to congratulate that gutsy kid," he said.

When he crossed the finish line, he regaled Maureen with encouraging words. She'd accomplished what he'd asked her to do—run the world's fastest women's marathon.

But in an interview with the *Toronto Star* after the race, and in his own personal account—which he composed on a typewriter with a blue ribbon—there's a sense that even he didn't totally understand the magnitude of her accomplishment.

He spent the majority of his own writing describing his personal struggle to finish all 26.2 miles. At one point, he said that of everything that had happened that day, "Perhaps the most astounding moment for me occurred when I added up the team totals and discovered that Geoff Wright, Bob Meharg, and I had won the second-place team prize." He told the newspaper reporter that Maureen was a "slow runner but truly phenomenal at the distances." That's an understatement. She wasn't just phenomenal. In that moment, she was the best *in the world*.

And yet, despite knowing her capabilities, he hadn't prepared anything special for Maureen if she broke the world record. His seeming lack of forethought is baffling. That afternoon, she received no medal and stood atop no podium. The only thing she got was a poster with a hand-drawn picture of Peter Tork, the bassist from Maureen's favorite band, the Monkees—a present from her teammate Carol Haddrall.

Maureen clutched the poster as Kathrine Switzer approached to offer congratulations. Kathrine had finished the race more than an hour slower than Maureen in 4:28:42. When she finished the Boston Marathon two weeks earlier, Kathrine knew right away that she'd just accomplished something important—historic. But this remote race in the sleepy suburbs of Toronto did not give her the same feeling. She asked Maureen how her race went. Maureen was more interested in talking about the Monkees, a subject far away from accusations of cheating and strange looks from adults.

After all, Maureen thought, *this was just a race*. She soon climbed into her mother's car and went home to shower. The family was headed to the cottage on Doe Lake.

***

At one A.M. the following Monday, Sy Mah's telephone rang. A journalist from London was on the other end of the line.

"We understand Maureen Wilton is only thirteen," the voice stated in a distinguished English accent. "And she bettered the world marathon record for women?"

Sy had been receiving calls like this all day Sunday and late into the evening Monday. Only one journalist and one photographer were at the marathon Saturday afternoon, but the story and images they filed had begun to spread around the world. In North York, a paper ran the headline "Toronto Girl, 13, Sets World Mark." Her time was front-page news on sports sections around Toronto.

For roughly twenty-four hours, Maureen remained oblivious. The family's cottage couldn't receive newspapers, and it didn't have a phone. Sunday morning, Maureen woke up and walked down the wooden steps on the cottage porch to do what she loved practically most in the world. She leaped into the lake. She didn't think about the weekend's events. It felt good to be back in the water, far, far away from the drama and cheating accusations of the previous day.

But as she basked in the Canadian spring air, journalists and sports officials in Toronto began analyzing and critiquing what she had done. Many people just assumed it was a hoax. Both Sy and Maureen's dad, Roger, were questioned about the validity of the record. Sy was asked if he was sure Maureen was a girl—a fact he had prepared for by getting a note from Maureen's doctor confirming *yes, she was a girl*, before the race. When Roger was asked how people could be sure she'd run the whole way, he cited the fact that course marshals meticulously watched and recorded every lap of the race.

Other men brushed off the accomplishment, believing it to be no big deal. The most powerful of them was Geoff Dyson, a pompous and respected British track coach who'd been brought across the Atlantic to help boost Canada's chances to succeed at the Olympics. Maureen's feat, he scoffed in the papers, "was like pushing peanuts up a hill with your nose"—a meaningless endeavor.

Ken Twigg, an official with the AAU who'd witnessed the marathon in person told reporters there was "nothing special in Wilton's time. If there's anything creditable here, it's that a young girl can finish a race." He failed to mention, of course, that the young girl came in sixth overall in the race, beating more than a dozen men.

Maureen returned home to North York and tried her best to ignore all the attention, which was difficult since a new article seemed to arrive daily. Her mom clipped out everything, even those with a negative tone.

Many articles did defend her achievement. A column in the sports section of Toronto's *The Mirror* stated, "Let's face it, no words, no matter what or who says them, will erase this brilliant performance by this North York girl."

Then there were the members of her club, who rallied together to honor the achievement. Gord Sim orchestrated a trophy presentation for Maureen days after the race, convincing Sy and other race organizers that her achievement was worthy of more recognition.

The words, both good and bad, piled up. And Maureen started to feel like she was a rope, being tugged back and forth between angry adults. She felt like she didn't have the ability to speak up for herself. She didn't want to disappoint anybody. She didn't want to be a controversy. She just wanted to run.

To cope, she started to diminish the race in her mind. If people didn't like what she'd done even though others had to come to her defense, well then, she was just going to pretend the whole thing wasn't a big deal. She was shy and she just didn't want to cause any trouble. She couldn't wait for the whole thing to blow over.

As the aftermath of the marathon simmered and then cooled down, Gord Sim made Maureen an elaborate plaque, atop which he bronzed her marathon shoe.

He also penned a poem in her honor that conveys the simple and meaningful appreciation and applause Maureen received from her teammates and their supporters:

Five runners have finished. Now Moe comes in sight.
She sprints the last mile like a rabbit in flight.
She's moved into sixth in remarkable style
To finish the grind with a six-minute mile ...
Mighty Moe.

19

Two weeks after the marathon, Maureen woke up in Detroit. Although the place was new, the routine was familiar, and there was comfort in that. Open your eyes in a strange house—the attic or basement or living room of whoever had agreed to board one, some, or all of the North York girls—get dressed, eat as much breakfast as you could stomach, pile into Sy's station wagon, and get to the track.

The day's event was at Lincoln Park High School. After three years of meets at various schools all over Canada and the United States, the buildings started to blend together. Lincoln Park had a single-story wing with a scalloped roof that connected perpendicularly to a brick-and-glass two-story section of the school— exactly the kind of structure that dissolved in Maureen's memory almost as fast as it appeared in her sight. The locations changed, but it was the race that mattered: the condition of the track, the competitors, her teammates, the distance, the pace. These elements felt particularly comforting after the events of the past few weeks.

Lincoln Park presented an arrangement of predictable

variables: a 1,000-yard race and a worthy competitor. Michigan State University's pentathlon champion Vann Boswell was six foot one to Maureen's four foot eight and a well-rounded collegiate athlete. Maureen was a recent world record holder in the marathon, but the feeling of that race was still on her legs, the heaviness of the controversy still present, unwelcome. Maureen performed better in longer races; the 1,000 was shorter than what she preferred. It wasn't exactly her distance. And yet, when it came time to compete, Maureen did what she had always done: She gave her all. In this event, with a time of two minutes and fifty-two seconds, it earned her first place.

Later that day, Maureen went on to compete with Sheila, Carol, and Brenda in the 4x880-yard team relay. Together they grabbed first place and set a record in Michigan for their 10 minute and 7.9 second finish in the two-mile event.

This wasn't just a good day; Maureen was ascendant.

In the upcoming months, she would sail through races that made spectators leap to their feet. Take the relay at the Carleton Place Centennial Celebrations—an event held each spring. The North York girls had swept every relay that they'd entered for the past two years. But on this occasion, for some reason, Sy filled two spots on the relay team with rookie runners. Then he tamped down the relay team's expectations. Right off the line, North York lagged. The first runner quickly fell to last place. This was what Sy had predicted. He knew deep down that this group was headed for a loss. And then it got worse. A spectator accidentally tripped the first North York runner, and the team lost a few more seconds right before the first handoff. Then, a surge. The second and third runners succeeded in getting North York into the top two. Finally, it was up to Maureen, who was the anchor—the team's final runner—to make up the ten-yard deficit. She took on the challenge with such athletic exuberance that spectators exploded into shocked applause. Despite running two other races that day, despite Sy's prediction that the group couldn't win against the competition, and despite a rocky start, Maureen delivered the team first place. She was Mighty Moe.

In June, Maureen was ready for another duel— against a record and the long-distance star and frequent North York competitor Roberta Picco. Earlier that year, Don Mills coach Lloyd Percival had staged a one-hour race at an indoor track to show off Roberta's incredible talent. It was a brand-new event where the goal was to run the farthest distance in sixty minutes. Sy tucked away the idea. And then, buoyed by Maureen's success at the marathon, Sy hosted his own hour event and invited Roberta to face off against Maureen.

The Saturday of the race, Maureen was more excited than usual. She knew Sy wanted her to beat the hour record, and there's no better motivation to run fast than a worthy competitor. Sure, Roberta had repeatedly beaten Maureen, but Maureen was on a tear. She was strong and confident. After covering 26.2 miles, running for only an hour (even if it was just loops around a track) seemed significantly less boring. Also: Thank goodness for speed. In this race, Sy assigned her a pace that felt right for the distance—zippy and hard, an *all the way to the limit* clip that Maureen had to work for.

Maureen arrived to the track at Northview Collegiate to find some five hundred boys and girls scheduled to participate in the day's events. Just like Lloyd had promoted his hour-long race in the papers, Sy had also publicly hyped the match. To her supreme disappointment, Roberta was a no-show. The Don Mills distance star was running a different race that weekend. In Roberta's place, a downpour arrived.

Summer showers were not uncommon in Toronto, but they were usually over quickly. This rain, however, was unrelenting. Within the first few laps of the one-hour race, runners found their rhythm splashing through ankle-deep puddles on the cinder-and-clay track.

Maureen's North York jersey was sopping, and her bangs stuck to her forehead, directing a stream of rain into her eyes. But the absolute worst was her shoes. They were engorged with water, and each step made an awful squeak. Thankfully, her Adidas weren't the only kicks creaking. The track was an uncomfortable chorus of soggy, noisy shoes.

Maureen saw the conditions as an equalizer. She wiped the drops from her eyes and held the pace that Sy had given her. And that discipline paid off. She ran nine miles and 165 yards, thought to be the world's fastest in the outdoor hour, beating both Brenda and Carol. (Roberta had run a bit more distance during Lloyd's event earlier that year, but her record was set indoors.) Sy was forced to cancel the remainder of the events because of the rain. Maureen's win closed out the day.

This time Maureen won the prize without the controversy. Finally, Maureen was free to be proud. She was thrilled over her first-place finish and tickled about her record. Even soaked to the bone, she felt better about this finish than her world record at the marathon, which was muddied by detractors. Bring on the literal mud, any day.

A coda to the event: Maureen had grabbed the record . . . to the best of Sy's knowledge. They found out only later that another runner at a different race had already run longer.

Even with the realization that she hadn't set a record, Maureen knew she'd persevered through awful conditions. She remained thankful that she was able to finish with pride.

At the Central Ontario Track-and-Field Championships in July, Maureen won a mile race in five minutes and 25.5 seconds. Her time was a Canadian record for her age bracket, sadly not recognized internationally due to the AAU's distance limits for women.

Maureen kept running. With every long run and every broken record, she proved that the regulations around the distances women could and couldn't complete were badly outdated. The rules and the attitudes of those who wrote them dramatically underestimated the capabilities of girls. Running's governing bodies were getting it wrong. In the 1960s, it wasn't just grumpy officials with an ax to grind. Public opinion wasn't much better.

**

Maureen's brother Dan and his friend Paul Mancuso walked out the south door of their high school during a break in class. They joined a loose collection of boys their age in the so-called "smokers' lounge." Now years past his brief stint as a runner, Dan smoked. Paul didn't. He hung around the smokers because he was friends with Dan. The break was brief, and the boys didn't usually talk about much—maybe about music or weekend plans.

But on this particular day, a short featherweight of an underclassman walked by. It was Maureen.

"Hey, look," said someone, nodding toward her. "That's the kid who set all those running records."

Dan and Maureen had always been close. He knew how hard she worked for those records. He was proud of her and protective. But Dan kept quiet, stayed still. The guys in the smokers' lounge didn't know that he and the running girl were related. In the poker game that is high school social interactions, Dan figured it would be easier for both him and Paul if they let the momentary blip in otherwise unimportant chatter pass.

"Does she even know that she's a girl?" another kid chimed in. The group chuckled as they exhaled their cigarette smoke.

On a normal day, with his red hair and fair skin, Dan blushed easily. But that comment about Maureen? Like red dye dropped in water. Paul observed his friend's anger transform him. Dan was radiating fury, his face a particularly bright color of rage.

Paul watched wide-eyed, wondering what would happen next. Would Dan storm away to fight a streetlamp? Was his head going to explode?

Miraculously, Dan held his tongue.

But this stupid comment in one Ontario high school was being repeated in one form or another all over

North America. In living rooms, newspaper articles, in letters, on porches, in regulatory meetings, the comments about women distance runners could get nasty: *They're pretending to be boys, they're going to grow chest hair, their ovaries are going to fall out, they won't be able to have children.*

Maureen didn't hear everything, but what she did hear stayed with her. She may have been running stronger than ever, but in the moments where her mind wasn't on her performance or school, the chatter about her sweatpants and her body lingered. She was an early teenager already sensitive to the ways she was changing. The weird glances and whispers only reinforced how different she felt. Sometimes, it was as if her body wasn't her own—just an object to be critiqued and judged.

So Maureen focused on what she could control: her pace, her effort, her drive. She lived for her time in the club, which usually felt like one of the only places she could really be herself. It was her safe place. Her home.

She had no idea that fissures were forming in its foundation.

20

For most kids Maureen's age, their lives revolved around school. School was where they acquired friendships and established their place in the social hierarchy, where they developed their taste in music and figured out what to do on the weekend. For Maureen, school was the thing she did before she got to her real life: the club.

In the club, there were adults—some Maureen liked, some she didn't—crushes, intense friendships, embarrassing moments, and events that changed you from a ten-year-old into a teen.

Stories became mythical, passed on to new members on road trips or after cooldowns. There was the time, in the early days, when John Penner pulled off his sweatpants and ran around the track in his underwear, completely unaware that he'd forgotten to put on his middle layer—his shorts. Or the day that Jo-Ann set off a stink bomb in the gym right before practice. Or the time the girls got in serious trouble for throwing snowballs at cars. (When one hit the fire chief's vehicle, Sy, who rarely showed anger, made the girls march over and apologize; the fire department was a big sponsor of the club.) Or the time Jo-Ann laughed so hard at one of Maureen's jokes that milk squirted from her nose, not once, not twice, but three times.

"You might as well go over and eat with the dogs," Jo-Ann's mom yelled after the white liquid squirted onto the table.

The girls would laugh about it for years.

Maureen went to see her first horror movie with Brenda. She went on her first double date with Jo-Ann. Around Christmas, the club held a formal dance at the Royal Canadian Legion hall. Parents, siblings, and runners gathered for the holiday celebration, and Sy handed out awards to runners. What Sy and Brenda and Maureen had built was not just a club but a tight-knit community for runners and their entire families.

Most days, Maureen's time with her friends existed in the moments between repeats, before races, or on late-night car rides. Any time the girls could spend longer stretches of time together was bliss.

During the summers, Jo-Ann and Maureen traded trips to each other's cottages. Maureen invited Carol to the cottage for a weekend of waterskiing and sleeping in bunk beds. When she met Carol at the nearest bus stop, Maureen hugged her and jumped around with glee.

The visit meant an enormous amount to Carol, too, who had never been anywhere like Maureen's family cottage before. She traveled for races, but that was it. Carol's mother didn't have money to get Carol running clothes, let alone a family car, vacation, or second home. But here was this inner-city girl, hanging out on a massive lake, Maureen's brother steering a boat, pulling the girls on water skis behind him.

Heaven, Carol thought, *this is heaven.*

For one week each summer, the entire team took a trip together. Sy organized a training camp where whole families would descend upon some lakeside location. They'd all camp and the parents would make food while the girls ran miles and miles in the wilderness or on sandy lake beaches. Between training camps, travel, and practices, the parents in the club also became quite close.

Sy took the girls out for a run sometimes twice a day, in the morning and then in the afternoon, or midday, if they were doing only one. Loping along, taking in the humid air filled with the smell of pine, dirt, and lake water, felt to Maureen like the right way to train. Not to mention that the people around her loved her. It was a safe space for sweatpants, not that she needed them in summer.

But the week wasn't exactly a beach vacation, either. The long runs at noon in the thick heat of summer were hard on runners like Sheila Meharg. Sheila's father would make sure to stop for a Popsicle on the way home.

One morning while driving caravan-style along Wasaga Beach on Georgian Bay, Maureen watched Sy's station wagon stop. The team was on their way to the first run of the day, and Maureen was in the car behind Sy's. From her window, Maureen saw Sy get out of his car and meet a few people who'd gathered in front of it on the beach.

Something wasn't right. The girls inside his station wagon stayed there. And Sy looked different. He didn't look like his usual breezy-but-focused self. For a minute he talked to the people in front of his car, and then the group disbanded. The beachgoers turned, and over one's arm was a limp puppy head just hanging. Maureen suddenly understood what she was seeing. The puppy had darted in front of Sy's car. And now the puppy was dead.

The caravan started up again and continued driving down the beach. When the girls got out, Sy delivered the instructions for the run. The girls trotted forward, feet squishing into the sand, dark blue lake on one side, dusty green trees on the other. Maureen couldn't focus on any of it. Her feet were moving, but her brain was a swamp, thick and heavy with the pain of that poor dog.

She ran the miles, picked at her food, and kicked around with the girls, but Maureen couldn't clear her mind of that puppy's face. Every time she thought about it, her throat clenched, her teeth pressed together, and a nauseating sinkhole opened in her chest like a wound. *That little head hanging.* She couldn't get over it.

A little later in the trip, someone suggested they go back to the same beach to run.

"I'm not going," said Maureen. "No way."

Maureen was usually a reliably light and bubbly presence in the group, especially during these training weeks. She was also not the kind of person to refuse to do something. If Sy told her to run a certain distance, she did it. When he told her to keep a certain pace, she closely monitored her strides. Whatever the race he planned for her, she would run it. So when Maureen said *no* with conviction, the rest of the team listened. They ran in a different location.

It didn't matter. For Maureen, the entire week was ruined, soaked in a sour memory that would forever make her stomach turn. It was not unlike the feeling she got when thinking about the marathon.

***

In the summer of 1968, when Maureen was fourteen years old, a surprising invitation arrived. It had been more than a year since Maureen's historic 26.2-mile run around York University, more than a year since her name was hidden in the five-mile lineup on the official program, more than a year since she endured puzzled looks from runners and ridiculous comments from race marshals. The officials at the Toronto Police Games promised Maureen something different. They invited Maureen and the girls at the North York Track Club to run a marathon *officially*.

In the United States, women were barred from running marathons. Women still weren't allowed to race distances longer than two miles. But now, in Canada, the Police Games Marathon was warmly and widely opening up its registration to women—which wasn't just a gesture, but a stark contrast to every other marathon that had come before it. A startling fifteen women were expected to run (a statistic proudly published in the papers), including North York Track Club's Maureen Wilton, Carol Haddrall, and Brenda Mah.

Sy hadn't trained the girls for the marathon this time around. They were already running between seventy and ninety miles a week. He didn't need to add more miles to their routine; their legs were ready. In the year since Maureen had broken the record, the time to beat had dropped by eight minutes. To claim a new record, the girls would have to run 26.2 miles faster

Moe with her brothers Gord (left) and Dan (right) at their first home in Toronto.

Maureen at her third birthday party.

Maureen at her parents' property on Doe Lake before they built their cottage.

Moe (left) with Brenda Mah (center) and Carol Haddrall (right) before a race.

Maureen in her yellow and burgundy North York Track Club uniform.

Mighty Moe running alongside John Penner, a high schooler several years older than her.

Maureen's parents were very supportive of her running.

In these stills from a Wilton home movie, Moe captures first place in a race and is congratulated by teammate Brenda, who has won a trophy of her own.

Scenes from various races. In the top image, Moe is wearing number 55. On the other starting line, she is in a crouch, third from right.

The girls on the North York Track Club quickly became one of the most dominant teams in North America. From left: Jo-Ann Rowe, Brenda Mah, Maureen, Eva Van Wouw, and Debbie Worrall.

Posing with her North York teammates before getting on a plane to Vancouver for the Canadian Cross Country Championships.

North York Track Club won the team prize at the Canadian and U.S. cross country championships. Top row from left: Carol, Sheila, Brenda. Bottom from left: Moe, Jo-Ann.

Maureen in 1966 surrounded by her team and their "hardware" from one race appearance.

Moe won more than a few ribbons. Here she is in front of her rapidly growing trophy collection.

In April 1967, Kathrine Switzer became the first woman to officially enter the male-only Boston Marathon—unbeknownst to race organizers. A few miles into the race, the race director tried to force her off the course, but was pushed aside by other runners. "I was embarrassed and humiliated," Switzer remembers. "At that moment . . . I knew that if I didn't finish the race, nobody would believe that women could do it or should be there." She finished in 4:20. These images spread around the world the next day, helping spark the fight for women's running equality.

Moe in training, c. 1967, at the Earl Haig High School track.

The official program for the Eastern Canadian Marathon Championships. Moe and Kathrine Switzer are not listed with the men. Instead, they appear in the "Women's Open 5 Miles." This was done to conceal the fact that they both planned to run the full 26.2-mile race.

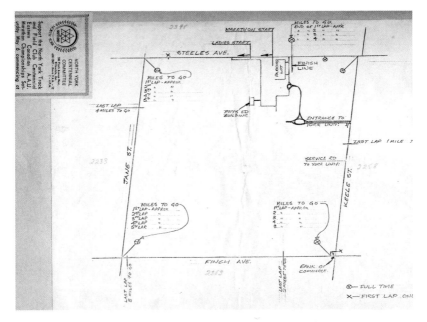

A hand-drawn map of the marathon course around the campus of York University. Runners completed five laps of the route—a boring course on paved roads in the northern suburb of Toronto.

At the starting line of the Eastern Canadian Centenniel Marathon Championships on May 6, 1967. Maureen, too nervous to line up next to the men minutes before the race, is not pictured. Kathrine Switzer, the only other female participant, is also not pictured.

Mighty Moe approaches a refreshment station in the middle of the marathon, paced by Carol Haddrall.

Mrs. Joan Sim gives Moe a drink of water at a refreshment station during the marathon.

Moe in the last stretch of the marathon, unsure whether or not she is going to beat the record. Her brother Gord (directly to her left) joins her for the surge, accompanied by his bandmates. Their van, with "The Spectrums" logo on the side, is visible in the background.

Facing page: The final sprint. Moe's last mile was completed in six minutes—a faster mile than any of the adult men ran that day.

After finishing the marathon, and breaking the world record, Moe poses with a drawing of Peter Tork from the Monkees— made for her by Carol Haddrall. This was the only award she received that day.

Moe poses for a photo with her parents Roger and Margaret after breaking the world record.

Days after the race, Moe returned to the finish of the race to receive a trophy made by Gord Sim, who is shaking her hand. Sy Mah stands behind her.

To Maureen:
Congratulations on a wonderful
& courageous effort that proves
girls are not the weaker sex
& that your fine coach was
perfectly correct in letting
you run. Good luck in
the years to come.
Lloyd Percival

A note Lloyd Percival, the coach of the Don Mills Track Club, sent to Maureen after her marathon record.

On March 13, 1968, Maureen was honored by the mayor of North York for her record-breaking marathon.

Kathrine Switzer and Maureen, reunited at the Goodlife Fitness Toronto Half Marathon in 2009.

Maureen and her mother, Margaret, supporting Moe's daughter, Carolyn, at a race in 2003.

Mighty Moe and her husband, Paul, with their two children, Anthony and Carolyn, in 2015.

than 3:07:26. But despite Sy's confidence in the girls, he curbed the public's expectations. This would not be a record-setting run. The reason: In the humidity and heat of mid-July, the girls would be unlikely to run as fast as they were capable. He predicted a three-hour, twenty-minute finish, tops.

Carol was excited. When she'd paced Maureen in the marathon the year prior, she'd wondered why she wasn't the one chosen for the historic race. She supported Maureen—*always*—but Carol was also a strong long-distance runner, with energy in her legs and confidence to know she could cover the distance. So when Carol got the opportunity to run a marathon a year later, she couldn't say *yes* fast enough.

Maureen, on the other hand, wasn't enthusiastic about the race. Even the word *marathon* set off a twisting in her stomach and a tightening in her chest. The distance and the awful things that had come afterward were inexorably tangled together. *And being accused of cheating!* Never in a million years had she even considered cutting corners, not in a marathon, not in anything. Sometimes she wished she'd never run that silly race in the first place.

But here she was again at the starting line of another marathon. This time around, in a small town northwest of Toronto, the start was a bit more scenic.

They gathered in a park with a gazebo. If she had to run it, she was thankful for Carol, Brenda, and the dozen or so other girls in the crowd who helped defuse the *"girls running a marathon"* spotlight that had made her feel so uncomfortable last time.

The first leg of the race took runners south toward Lake Ontario. Carol disappeared in the small crowd ahead of Maureen. Maureen ticked off the miles with relative ease. Sy *had* prepared them for this. But working against her was a force unlike one she'd ever encountered during a race. Maureen just didn't want to be there. The force didn't slow her down, but it did make her every move more tedious.

They ran on a sidewalk adjacent to the highway for miles. As Carol ran, she realized that she didn't have a clear understanding of the distance. Like Maureen, she also arrived that day because Sy told her to. She trusted Sy to know what she was capable of, and she didn't consider that this race was different. But this run next to a freeway was starting to feel . . . long.

When Carol passed fifteen miles, she passed the farthest distance she had ever run. The temperature had begun to rise. The heat was the kind you get from two directions: beamed down on you from above and radiated up at you from the concrete below.

Carol passed tables covered with paper cups filled

with water. She didn't see them as hydration stations; she saw them as unnecessary pit stops that would slow her down. She passed each one without easing off her stride. Never in any of her training had she learned about the importance of salt and water—and just how much of each you lose when you sweat. As she ran, she tangled with dehydration and muscle cramps. She challenged the cells in her body to function properly without two essential ingredients because she refused to forfeit speed.

Carol turned left onto Lake Shore Boulevard, which bordered Lake Ontario. If Lake Shore Boulevard offered a scenic break from the monotony of the highway or slightly cooler temperatures because of the lake, Carol didn't notice. It was mile eighteen and she was focused on her legs, which were starting to seize up. She still had eight miles left to run. Eight miles is a whole track practice. Eight miles is more than the width of the city of San Francisco. Eight miles . . . well, Carol started to worry that it wasn't a distance she could cover with legs in full revolt.

"Carol!"

She turned her head. There was Sy trotting toward her from behind. Carol let everything in her head spill out to her coach at once.

"I have cramps in my legs. I can't stop them from spasming. I don't think I can finish."

Sy slowed down to match Carol's pace, waving on the men running with him.

"Go ahead," she said to Sy, thinking he would leave her. But her coach didn't change pace and didn't say a word. Carol, like the other girls on the team, was an extremely hard worker. He'd also seen her threaten to quit. She was, after all, the one known for throwing herself down on the grass after a long practice and declaring confidently, "Coach, I quit!" only to be pulled back like a magnet the next day. Sy knew better than to think Carol was capable of giving up. He also knew that the marathon was no standard-issue race.

Five miles to the finish, Carol ran with her toes pointed up in the air like an elf, afraid that any other position would nudge her feet into a cramp. (Her legs were already goners.) However hilarious her stride, Carol held on to the familiar rhythm of her feet hitting the pavement. After what seemed an unreasonable amount of miles, Carol and Sy reached the Canadian National Exhibition Stadium, a massive facility with a track and bleachers stretching far higher than you'd expect for a modest marathon. As Carol passed through the entrance, a group from the North York Track Club was waiting.

Carol was the kind of runner who didn't like cross-country races because she couldn't see the finish line through the trees. But finally, after twenty-five-plus miles, she could see it: One lap of the track and she'd be done.

Someone in the stadium offered her water, and she turned it down. The man dumped the whole bottle on her.

What the hell! She turned and gave him a glare. *Screaming legs, elf toes, and now this?*

Just a final ninety, seventy, fifty yards to go when Sy suddenly slowed. Carol turned, confused. Then it hit her: He wanted her to cross the finish line alone.

When she did, after three hours and thirty minutes, she received a few quick shocks.

First, she saw her mother and two younger sisters standing in the grass next to the track. In two years, it was the first race or practice that her mother had ever attended. It wasn't that her mother didn't care, but with raising five girls on her own, a job, and no car, the freedom to attend her daughters' extracurriculars was hard to come by.

Second, she learned she was the first female finisher. She'd won the women's race.

Third, she doubled over from the pain of severe cramping in one of her legs.

"Are you okay?" asked a sister.

And then Carol reached for the other leg, which was

suddenly just as painful as the first. Carol screamed and fell to the grass. The medical team rushed over and carried her to an ambulance, where they massaged Carol's cramped legs and feet and got her hydrated. In twenty minutes, she was transformed from a spasming knot of an athlete into a regular sore one. As she strode back to meet her mother, she stood tall. Carol Haddrall was the first official (key word: *official*) female finisher—not just of this race, but of any marathon in North America.

It was a distinction that was lost on her. Sy may have realized it when he held back in the last fifty yards of the race, the same way he knew what he was doing when he staged the marathon for Maureen, but he didn't let the girls in on his strategy. Their job was to run.

And run they did. In another North York Track Club domination, Maureen finished second and Brenda finished third.

When Carol took the stage that evening to accept her trophy in a gold dress her mother had borrowed from a friend, the men who ran the marathon gave her a standing ovation. She didn't understand why they were standing. She knew a few of them, but not all of them. They seemed to understand what she hadn't yet grasped—and what neither she nor Maureen would understand fully for another fifty years: that their achievements were of historical importance, not just in the race itself, but to the future of women in the sport.

***

By the end of the summer, Sy had the girls run two more marathons.

Maureen's legs worked fine, but the tide of mental fatigue, burnout, and boredom was rising.

"I don't really want to run this," Maureen said to her mom in the middle of the Boardwalk Marathon, a summer race held along the lake just east of Toronto.

"Well, just finish it."

Sigh. "Okay."

Maureen took first place. But she didn't enjoy it.

21

Increased public scrutiny. Relentless training.
Marathoning fatigue. If, in the summer of 1968, the
below-the-surface fissures in Maureen's running life
and the club started to expand slowly, the fall of 1968
cracked everything open with a magnitude-six earth-
quake and months' worth of aftershocks.

The shattering news came suddenly, like most earth-
quakes, on a peaceful day before a normal practice.

Sy was leaving the club.

For nearly five years, since Maureen was ten, Sy Mah
had been the architect of her running life. Whether she
ran fast or slow during workouts and races, his hand
was on the dial. In fact, he had designed that dial. Every
weekend, they traveled to the places he wanted them
to travel. They ran the races he wanted them to run.
They practiced through injury and illness because he
told them to.

But in return for Maureen's extreme dedication, she
got someone who saw her as an athlete. Someone who
recognized her unique strengths as a distance runner
and designed opportunities to test them.

Sy had come to running late. He didn't get into the sport until his late thirties. But once he got into it, he gave it everything—his weekends, his daughters, his free time. Maureen's own enthusiasm was a match for his. *Want to run ten miles to get to a race? Sure thing.* Maureen didn't collapse after each practice; she begged for more. Sy valued her can-do spirit because he had the same.

Each girl in the club had her own relationship with Sy. For Maureen, his belief in her and his steady support acted as an invisible framework that supported her running.

And then, out of nowhere, that framework disappeared.

In the days and weeks following the announcement that Sy was leaving, the concrete details were hard for Maureen to hold on to.

Sy was going to Toledo, Ohio. He was taking a postgraduate course on exercise science. He could no longer be in charge of the club. First it seemed like he would be commuting down to Ohio weekly. Then Maureen heard that he was leaving Canada entirely. Rumors flew that his family was in disarray. The details enlarged and twisted in her mind, as she probed for answers that wouldn't come.

Sy hoped that the club would carry on without him.

But could Maureen?

Then came the aftershocks.

With Sy went Brenda, suddenly and without ceremony. Just like that, the two people who'd welcomed Maureen into the club, who'd provided motivation, friendship, competition, and support were gone. Brenda had taken a small break before, a rebellious little detour of adolescence that didn't include running. But she came back. Maureen knew this time was different. The friend she chased to her first ribbon, her first win, her first international race, was gone in what felt more like a tragedy than a goodbye.

The aftershocks didn't stop. Carol's departure started with a bum knee. When Carol mentioned her pain to Sy, he brushed it off. "Kill it to cure it," he said. So Carol limped around the track, powering through the pain. And for her grit and determination, Carol landed in the doctor's office with a torn meniscus. Her running, specifically following the training and the schedule that Sy designed for her, had ripped her cartilage apart. His exit from the club took place while she was recovering.

Injury was something that Maureen had witnessed before. It took her friends, but usually she got them back. Sy's intentions may have been good, but his "never say die" mentality, paired with a lack of knowledge about injury prevention, put the girls in his club at serious risk of injury. Sy had sent Carol forward as proof that girls could run. And she proved it over and over until her body couldn't prove it anymore.

Just three weeks after a doctor cut open Carol's knee, and with the incision still tender, Carol laced up her shoes for a race. Sy may have been gone, but his methods were embedded. Carol's knee ached after the event and the location of the tear still throbbed. Instead of taking a few more weeks at home to recover, she returned to the track at Earl Haig. For a while, Carol got rides home. She was in no state to walk more than an hour home each night after practice. But soon, her situation in the club became unsustainable. She was hurt and lived too far away.

Maureen didn't see Carol again.

Her coach, her first running partner and friend, her honorary big sister: all gone in a matter of weeks. The whole thing didn't feel right—not their departures, training, traveling, or competing. When Maureen had had disappointments in the past, she steadied herself with the act that brought her joy: In running she found peace and she felt freedom. So Maureen stuck to the routine of practicing and racing, waiting for those feelings she could always rely on to return. But the loss of her friends and her coach felt like a wound. And one additional consequence of Sy's departure made it sting.

***

Peter Mason.

If the club was going to continue, it needed a new coach. Parents, club members, and advisors unanimously voted to elevate Peter, a thin, bespectacled, absentminded-professor type who'd assisted Sy with the team since not long after Maureen started. He had the credentials to take over one of the most prestigious running clubs in the country. Peter taught at Rippleton Road Public School and for three years had organized track-and-field meets for North York public schools. That was on top of the years he'd spent as assistant coach to the North York Track Club. Peter wasn't as gregarious as Sy. He certainly wasn't as press-savvy. But he did carve out a place for himself in the club.

Sheila remembers getting ready for an indoor half-mile race with several of her North York teammates. Sy always wanted the girls to run to win, but on this particular day, he instructed the team to run together. It was almost as if on this rare occasion, the goal was to show off the club's prowess, not the power of an individual runner. Peter didn't agree with the strategy. He quietly took Sheila aside and told her to "get in front and stay there." It meant ignoring Sy's instructions.

When it came time to run, Sheila listened to Peter. She attacked the course and held nothing back. Sheila didn't just win the race, she set a new record.

Sheila was thrilled, but she worried about Sy's reaction. Trusting in her coach's strategy was the way races were done. And in this event, she didn't listen. To Sheila's great relief, Sy was pleased, not disappointed.

But Peter did not take Maureen aside and tell her to give it her all. He didn't give her personalized pep talks or big warm congratulations after a good race. He did not joke around with her like Sy did. In fact, Maureen got the distinct impression that Peter didn't like her very much.

Exhibit A: car rides. If she rode in Peter's car to or from a race, he'd report back to her parents that she didn't behave. Maybe it was all the singing? But she wasn't the only one rattling off "Ninety-nine Bottles of Beer on the Wall" or crooning to the Beach Boys or the Beatles on the radio. She didn't understand why she routinely got in trouble.

Her parents listened to Peter's reports with extreme skepticism. They were friendly with the other parents in the club, most of whom adored Maureen and were utterly charmed by her. Apart from the snowball incident, she'd never gotten in real trouble. And then there was the fact that Peter was never particularly friendly with Maureen's parents. They didn't make small talk or strategize about Maureen's running. Margaret was a fierce protector of her daughter, and it bothered her that she could never get a straight answer from Peter about what Maureen had done to prompt his irritation.

Exhibit B (and in Maureen's opinion, this was worst of all): Peter motivated other girls in the club by telling them to go after Maureen. Sy firmly believed that when the girls competed hard against one another, they competed at their best. It was a sort of "we all improve when one of us improves"–type approach, and it felt right to Maureen. Peter, on the other hand, played favorites. He tried to motivate one girl to win by taking another one down. It was entirely antithetical to Maureen's approach to competition. But more than that, what was happening in the club seemed to upset the balance between two prominent (and seemingly at odds) features of her personality: Maureen was both a fiercely loyal friend and also fiercely competitive.

These two parts of her wouldn't seem to jive considering that all Maureen's closest friends also raced against one another. In competition, a clock literally measured Maureen's performance and compared it with her teammates'. Running isn't a team sport. Only one person gets to cross a finish line first. In a very traditional sense, the winner succeeds only if her friends fail.

But Maureen never saw her drive to win as a drive for others to lose. From the beginning, the club fostered a kind of symbiosis between friendship and running. "Champions make champions," as Sy said. Brenda's running inspired Maureen, and it motivated her to work harder. And this standard of cooperation and competition set the tone for other girls who joined the club. Like Brenda giving Maureen one of her trophies or Carol running with Maureen during Maureen's first marathon despite also wishing she could run it, the girls supported one another's efforts to get better. They recognized and admired one another's unique talents—the ones who sprinted, the ones who could kick to the finish, the ones, like Maureen, who could endure.

Yes, they ran against one another, but they also ran for one another. They made one another fast. They made one another proud. Maureen's wins were not in spite of her teammates' efforts, but because of them.

At a race you line up next to a cluster of other people, but running is really a competition against your past self—the person you were a day ago, a month ago, a year ago. Maureen could never see her, but she was there at the starting line of every race, too—the girl who ran yesterday and the day before that and the day before that. Maureen knew what she looked like, what she was thinking, how she felt, and how fast she finished. She knew what made her doubt and what made her strong. She knew everything she needed to beat her.

Every step forward on a run meant Maureen was getting a little better—a little farther ahead of the girl she used to be. That's not a metaphor. That's just how running works.

Which is why, whenever Maureen stood next to her friends on a starting line in Ottawa or Baltimore or High Park, she never thought she was competing *against* them. In her mind, she competed *with* them, powered by them. They all had their own races to win.

For nearly five years, these two pillars of her personality—intense friendship and intense competition—made running with the North York Track Club the great passion of Maureen's life. They were the moments of the sharpest focus, the purest enjoyment, the clearest memories: wet leaves and burning quads on the Burnett hills, jumping through sprinklers and laughing with Jo-Ann, sharing a can of corned beef and bread in a hotel room with Carol or wonton soup with Sy, slopping through ankle-high puddles for one soaking hour. Maureen was her truest self in the club. *Was.* Until those pillars started to crumble, compromising the structure she'd worked so hard to uphold.

Friends left and the club's definition of competition became more straightforward, at least for Maureen: one teammate who tries to beat another. They were no longer running in the same direction; they were fighting in opposite ones.

22

The people who browsed the sports section in the local paper over morning cups of coffee would never know about North York Track Club's behind-the-scenes personal drama. Sy's departure was published in the paper, but it was reported as the passing of the torch, not the extinguishing of the flame. So as the residents of Toronto crinkled the thin paper while they skimmed through the morning's news, it appeared as though Maureen Wilton was running better than ever.

In December, just a few months after the shake-up, Maureen was one of six young Canadian women invited to an elite training camp in Edmonton, Alberta. The Canadian Track and Field Association chose her as one of the runners with "the potential and ability to become a great athlete." In other words, after nearly five years of running, Maureen was on the national radar as one of Canada's best. She was fifteen years old. It had been almost two years since her world-record-breaking marathon, and her status in the sport continued to climb.

But what did that mean? The Olympics were not an option. The 800 was still the longest distance available to women, and Maureen's strength was measured in miles, not meters. However, Maureen was poised for the international stage in events without such rigid distance limitations.

In the spring, Maureen got her chance. She entered a two-mile qualifier race for the 1969 International Cross-Country Championships, to take place in Scotland. The catch: She had to run against her old rivals Roberta Picco and Abby Hoffman. Abby was already an Olympian; she competed as an 800-meter runner in both the 1964 and 1968 games. Abby closed races with a commanding finish. Roberta let Maureen get closer, on occasion, but Maureen had never quite managed to squeak ahead when it counted.

Maureen and Jo-Ann were giddy with the idea of running overseas. There were two spots open to women in eastern Canada, and they wished for an outcome that would nab them spots one and two. But to do it, they'd have to face the most accomplished competition in the region.

The day of the qualifier, Jo-Ann sat in her car, hands balled up with anxiety. Maureen's bubbly demeanor quieted as the pressure of the race—the culmination of five years of work—settled on her.

Sweats off. Legs swinging. A white line on a track. Lean. Crack! *Run.*

Jo-Ann dropped behind a handful of women almost immediately. In fact, she'd begun sweating even before the start. She'd woken up with body aches and a fever, a sickness she knew well. She'd had cold after cold after cold for the last few years, so her body's rebellion was not surprising, but certainly disappointing. "Never say die," Sy always said. She figured the worldview still applied, even in his absence, even when her lungs were on fire and her whole body hurt more than her legs.

Maureen kept her eyes on Abby Hoffman's impossibly long strides. Her legs seemed to take one step for Maureen's every three; they inspired her to keep up. She dug in with every breath. Her arms rotated around her, only slightly bent, held away from her body as if a pillow were stuck between her abdomen and elbows.

A run that hard tends to empty the mind, but in flashes Maureen wondered about Roberta. She was typically a steady presence just in front of Maureen. But where was she now? Maureen pushed ahead, knowing at any second Roberta's own long legs would appear next to her.

But Roberta was behind in this race. Maureen didn't know it, but the track star had quit running competitively in 1968 when she entered university. A guidance counselor had persuaded Roberta to stop training seriously months earlier, suggesting school was a safer choice for her future. She couldn't pass up an opportunity to qualify for an international race, but when Roberta lined up to compete for Scotland, she was recovering from an Achilles injury and out of racing shape.

Abby crossed the line with a two-mile time of eleven minutes and fifty-two seconds, claiming first. Maureen came in second fourteen seconds later. Roberta finished thirty-four seconds behind Maureen to claim fifth, just ahead of Jo-Ann, who finished with a fever and sixth place.

Maureen became an official member of the Canadian National Team bound for the International Cross-Country Championships in Scotland. She would wear Canada's official red-and-white tracksuit. She would fly over the Atlantic Ocean with the best runners of her country to compete against the best runners in the world.

***

As she stood in the airport waiting for her plane, wearing a trench coat and holding a black purse, her hair curled, Maureen understood the magnitude of this accomplishment. Yet again, her membership on this team brought her more pride than breaking the world record in the marathon. She smiled tentatively as her parents took pictures of her departure. She wasn't the "real shrimp" of her early days on the track or even the

"Little Moe" of the marathon. She was "Mighty Moe" now, and it was time to take her place on the world stage.

Maureen boarded the plane without any of her North York teammates. She watched the brilliant green, yellow, and blue tapestry of the ground below as the plane glided past the eastern edge of Canada and over the Atlantic. Maureen closed her eyes and woke up in Scotland in the morning. The chill in the damp air crawled inside her coat. It was technically spring, but the trees were still bare. Maureen visited an outdoor market and bought a wool sweater. She took blurry pictures of the men's seven-and-a-half-mile race. She captured them, in muted colors, running up rolling hills of grass.

When it was Maureen's turn to run, she pulled on her red-and-white shorts and singlet under a red-and-white Canada sweatsuit. She tied her shoulder-length hair in a ponytail. She ran the 2.5-mile course of shallow hills with a few steep climbs. The weather was atrocious. Muck splattered across her legs as she trudged through the rainy bog. She was outmatched, but it didn't much matter. She came in thirty-first place. She was still honored to run for Canada and glad to have taken the trip.

***

Maureen had lost her momentum. Sy Mah always had another race planned, another road trip scheduled, another scheme up his sleeve. But he was gone.

Back from Scotland, Maureen stood on the Earl Haig track preparing to run another lap. She shook out her legs, swung her arms, leaned forward, ground her front toe into small stones, and ... *nothing.* She felt nothing. These moments used to fill her to the brim—leap from her as soon as she got to the track. Running with the club made Maureen feel both jubilant and focused, nervous and excited. The competition fueled her; her talented friends in the club motivated her to work harder. But for six months, her ties to the club had begun to loosen. It was imperceptible at first. The events in the fall felt like a loss that she could recover from. If she just waited long enough, the things she loved about the club would return. So Maureen kept running, holding on tightly to who she was. She marveled at competitors. Congratulated friends and teammates on their wins. And rededicated herself to training and racing.

But the sport stopped giving back to her in return. Like sore muscles that get better only to reveal an injury, Maureen's feelings about running and the club went deeper than that initial grief. Her style of loyalty and competition—those two pillars of her personality that had worked together for so long—was no longer supported by the North York Track Club. Which affected Maureen's running. Not the act of running, but the feelings associated with it. Her life's biggest passion had transformed into a hollow physical act—one that swallowed all her time, stressed her out, and alienated her from other people her age. All Maureen had ever wanted to do was run. But the messy, convoluted, unjust parts of life got in the way. Accusations of cheating, critics in the newspapers and in her neighborhood, a coach who offered her up to prove a point, another coach who valued competition over friendship.

Margaret noticed all this before Maureen did.

So, as Maureen was watching her teammates run, Margaret strolled up beside her. She looked at her daughter and paused.

Maureen was tired. Not the kind of up-all-night-driving-to-a-race sort of tired, but the five-years-of-nonstop-running-under-extreme-pressure sort of tired.

"Are you enjoying yourself?" Margaret asked.

"Not really," Maureen said in a flat tone.

"Maybe it's time to quit."

Maureen could think of no reason to disagree.

In the summer of 1969 Maureen and her mom left practice. They did not come back.

23

There's this very brief moment that happens right after you cross the finish line of a race. Your body has given everything to the effort out on the course, and as you take a few deep breaths, your shoulders drop, hips relax, heartbeat slows. There's no more strategy spinning through your brain. In stillness, you feel the endorphins flush through your nervous system. Your body has done the work. Then your brain takes control again. And you start to reflect on everything that just happened. That brief moment is over.

Maureen had the same feeling of release after she quit.

The previous five years had been a relentless pursuit of perfection—more ribbons, more trophies, better placement, more events, new cities, longer runs, more impressive records. Just as Maureen hit one goal, she was encouraged to reach for another—sometimes on the same day. Sometimes when people didn't want her to.

Opening the door to women's running equality

required a battering ram. Someone like Maureen, who could pound again and again even though it hurt, even though it sometimes seemed futile. Maureen never saw the door bust open.

When she stepped away from that challenge, she stopped reading the sports section, lost touch with girls who stayed in the club, didn't so much as inquire what races were happening that weekend or who was breaking records. That part of her life was over. She turned away from running completely.

And, in some ways, running turned away from her. There was no article announcing her departure. No journalist came knocking, asking why a former world record holder suddenly quit when she seemed to be peaking at a national level. When younger girls from North York traveled to Michigan for a meet, a team from Michigan asked where Maureen was. They'd been training hard to catch up to her. The North York girls told the other team that Maureen had quit. There wasn't any more mention of her.

The split from the sport was so profound, Maureen could look at her life in two pieces: when she was running and when she quit running.

Here's what happened after she quit:

Maureen did not talk about running.

She did not think about running.

All of a sudden, she had ... time—hours and hours to herself. Maureen had free afternoons, she could sleep in on the weekends, she could read, or listen to music at home without having to rush off anywhere.

So she did things that other kids her age did: She sang in the school choir and had small parts in school plays like *Bye Bye Birdie* and *Oklahoma!* She watched her brother Gord's band, the Spectrums, practice in the garage. She became a regular fixture at his shows.

Her parents, though, were devastated. Margaret and Roger were fierce believers in Maureen's abilities, and it was hard to watch her walk away from something she had once loved so much. Maureen's community had become their community. But they also understood how the pressure and the changes in the club had affected Maureen. More than anything, they wanted their daughter to be happy.

After Maureen's life changed, theirs did, too. Without the additional financial burden of sending her daughter to races, Margaret quit the job at Eaton's. She traded it for a secretarial job at Maclean Hunter, which offered regular weekday hours and wide-open weekends for the first time in years.

But for Maureen, the greatest concrete benefit

of quitting the club was that she could spend more time at the cottage. Instead of squeezing in a visit here and there on Sundays, after a race or when Margaret was off work, Maureen was free to stay up all weekend. Swimming, hiking, and spending time in nature felt all the more delicious without an impending race.

***

Two years go by, and Maureen finishes high school. She walks proudly across the graduation stage in a white gown and Mary Jane shoes. In the picture of the graduating class, Maureen is in the front row, one of a few dozen. If you didn't know her face, she'd be hard to pick out from the crowd.

There is a lot of uncertainty about what will happen next. She loves animals, nature, and music, but those aren't practical paths to adulthood. She had a great passion once, but that is gone now. Most of the jobs she considers feel like a cloudy mix of mediocre.

"What do you want to do?" her mother asks.

"I don't know," says Maureen.

Forever practical, Margaret has a suggestion: "Well, let's look at the paper and see what kinds of jobs are available."

They scan the classified listings, and they see one

job appear over and over: legal secretary. So Maureen signs up for a course at a community college that will prepare her for the job in the paper. She hates it. She has "zip, zero, nada" interest in what she's learning. One year in, she drops out.

Maureen gets an entry-level job at a publishing company correcting mislabeled subscriber addresses. Her coworkers move around her with no knowledge of who she was or what she's done. Maureen certainly doesn't tell them.

She takes her grandma to the opening night of the movie *The Exorcist* and walks out before it's over with haunting visions she wishes she could forget. Leaving the theater, her grandma says: "Thanks anyway, dear."

Maureen attends a weeklong water-ski-jumping summer camp. For as steady and confident as she felt on foot and even on water skis, she finds flying off a ramp propelled forward by a boat terrifying and unsettling. She quickly learns what not to do. *If you so much as breathe on that ramp, you're upside down.* Maureen tries to stay steady. But after four days of wobbling, falling, and skidding over the ramp, Maureen resigns herself to the feeling that the sport doesn't come naturally to her. *This is just not my thing.*

Maureen packs up before the final day of camp and heads home. She tells people, "I had to quit while I was still alive."

But even as Maureen moves on without mentioning her life before, a few people know. Even if they don't talk about it, it brings a kinship. Maureen keeps in touch with Jo-Ann, who also quit the club.

While driving with friends to the movies, Jo-Ann got back spasms so badly that she shrieked in agony. It wasn't the first time. For months she'd been struggling with persistent pain in her back—a pain so extreme that she started bending farther and farther forward until her short frame was curled up like a fern frond. She was a sixteen-year-old hunchback. Jo-Ann could not escape surgery this time. She needed a procedure called a spinal fusion that would bind her vertebrae together. Jo-Ann's health forced her to quit the club. As her body broke down, so did Jo-Ann's Olympic hopes. Overtraining was to blame. She vowed never to compete in a race again.

Carol, Sheila, and Brenda disappear from Maureen's life entirely.

Sheila also quits, although Maureen doesn't know it. In high school, the three-mile record holder started to get interested in art and music. She relaxed her training a little bit and started taking it easier in practices. Peter

Mason took her aside and told her that she was putting on too much weight, that she should cut back on all the ice-cream sundaes. The comment didn't bother Sheila too much, because by that point she'd grown tired of competing.

The heart of the club was gone. Most of the girls quit well before they reached college.

Later on, from his new life in Ohio, Sy would wonder if his training methods were too extreme. "I feel kind of badly about it. I wish I had emphasized it more— keeping fit for life. But I was a coach like other coaches, and we wanted good performances. Now I tell everyone this is good for your health and it's for life. But that wasn't known in those days."

***

And then there's Paul. Paul Mancuso, who grew up poring over the sports pages, who read about Maureen's every record. Paul, who was a close friend of Dan's and the Spectrums' biggest fan. Maureen met Paul in eighth grade. He'd been over to the house and even visited the cabin. But at Dan's college graduation party, things feel different between them. At this party, he isn't just a person who hung around with Maureen's brother. He is a person with a soft-spoken kindness, someone who knows Maureen— both the runner and nonrunner—and likes her.

Paul leaves the next day to work at a summer camp for boys, and Maureen and Dan go to visit for a day. Paul and Maureen write letters to each other all summer. They start dating. When Maureen is twenty-one, she and Paul get married. Jo-Ann dances the jive at Maureen's wedding with joy, athleticism, and skill, flipping in the air and spinning with her partner, just as you'd expect her to.

Maureen and Paul honeymoon at the cottage. They adopt two shelter dogs, a golden retriever and a poodle mix they name Sandy and Brandy. The dogs make Maureen and Paul's house a home.

Sandy and Brandy keep each other company while Paul teaches and Maureen goes to work. She becomes one of eighteen tellers at a big Canadian bank in a well-trafficked mall. Over the fifteen years she works there, she comes in contact with hundreds of thousands of customers who smile and deposit checks or withdraw their money. Not one understands who Maureen is. Customers walk away with no inkling that standing before them was the first woman to run a marathon in Canada. They have no idea that at age thirteen, that same woman held the world record in the marathon.

Maureen and Paul buy a cottage just down the lake from Maureen's parents' place. Then they buy a two-bedroom house in North York. Eventually, they sell their house in the suburbs for a bigger one.

When Maureen is thirty-six years old, she has her first child. They name the girl Carolyn. Their son, Anthony, arrives three years later. Maureen stays home with the kids. She's now spent more of her life without running than with it. That five-year period recedes in her memory. She indulges herself by watching track and field during the Olympics, but otherwise she completely shuts off her interest in the sport. Maureen doesn't mention running to her friends, her neighbors, or her children. Paul, knowing how she feels about bragging, never mentions it, either.

She meets a dear friend while working at the bank, one she cherishes. Others dip in and out of her life. But none are forged with the intensity of the friendships she made in the club, a cohort fused together by a trailblazing passion and persistent controversy.

Maureen's brothers die. First Dan, then Gord. They go for different reasons, but both too soon. Maureen loses her father, too.

When she thinks about who she is, Maureen returns to her love of nature, of her children, and her dogs. But in the world, she feels odd—like her interests have never quite aligned with most people's.

Running is pushed so deep into the corners of her brain that she almost never thinks about it. And when she does, she doesn't see the value of those years beyond her own experience in them. Sure, she won some races and amassed several bookshelves of trophies and ribbons, but other girls did, too. She doesn't see herself as special. Her triumphs were controversial and forgotten.

So she keeps her scrapbooks packed away, her trophies in boxes in the basement. Over time, the little gold figurines snap off from their bases. The dozens upon dozens of first-, second-, and third-place trophies break under the weight of life stored in boxes above. That five-year slice of her life is broken, folded up, and kept out of sight.

24

Over the years, Maureen wondered if she should
throw away the moldering boxes of trophies in the basement. The collection of ribbons, plaques, and mounted
figurines took up space, hiding in jumbled broken piles
inside withering cardboard.

For four decades she lived her life kind of like one
of those trophies. A star in the dark, as far away from
public display as possible. The fact that she once broke
the world record for a women's marathon? She didn't
think it was a big deal. She figured nobody cared. For
decades, she thought her record-breaking time on May
6, 1967, had dissipated into nothing.

She was wrong.

***

After the record fell, Dr. Ernst van Aaken noticed. Based
in West Germany near the Dutch border, van Aaken
looked a bit like a mad scientist. He had a widow's peak,
giving him a large, pronounced forehead, and short
tufts of hair on top of his head that seemed to defy a

comb's wishes. Instead of a white lab coat, though, van Aaken preferred a tracksuit.

The doctor, an avid runner and the leader of a track team called the Olympic Sport Club, based in Waldniel, his hometown, believed that the most effective way for distance runners to get faster was to run longer and run slower.

"Run many miles, many times your racing distance if you are a track runner," he advised.

This theory was radical at the time. The best track athletes in the world made intervals—those short bursts of speed repeated over and over—a key part of their training. Many runners were wary of what so many miles would do to their bodies. But van Aaken persisted, training the athletes in his club with his method. And they started to win—all over the world.

But van Aaken wasn't done. He firmly believed women could thrive under his long-and-slow mileage method—not just able to complete a marathon, but to do it nearly as fast as the men.

So when the astonishing news arrived in West Germany that a thirteen-year-old Canadian girl named Maureen Wilton had broken the women's world record in the marathon, journalists were skeptical, but van Aaken was a believer. Van Aaken was not only persuaded by the reports of this thirteen-year-old girl, but he defended her accomplishments to journalists, who thought the record must have been some hyperbolic achievement mistranslated as it traveled across the Atlantic. For his stance on Maureen's time, van Aaken was mocked and ridiculed—just an odd doctor from the boonies. So he decided to offer his country irrefutable proof that women could run the distance fast. He organized a marathon and invited women to compete.

On September 16, 1967, two women, a twenty-seven-year-old middle-distance runner and mother of two named Anni Pede and a nineteen-year-old named Monika Boers, gathered on a street in Waldniel with a few dozen men. The race angered Germany's version of the Amateur Athletic Union, but the organization eventually relented, stipulating that women could run so long as they started the race thirty minutes after the men.

Four months after Maureen's world record, Anni Pede finished van Aaken's marathon in 3:07:26. She beat Maureen's time by eight minutes, becoming the new marathon world record holder and proving to Germans that women could not only run the marathon, but run it well.

The mad scientist had his vindication, and athletes and officials around Germany began to rethink the limitations they put on women's running. By 1971, German organizers opened up the marathon to women officially. And two years later, van Aaken hosted the first women's-only marathon in the world.

***

On December 5, 1971, the women's marathon record fell again, this time to a woman named Cheryl Bridges. Two years previous, Maureen had crossed paths with the American distance phenom. She and Maureen both ran on the same muddy Scottish hills at the 1969 International Cross-Country Championships, but Cheryl, a twenty-one-year-old from Indianapolis with striking blond hair, ran for the United States and claimed fourth place, and Maureen, fifteen at the time, ran for Canada and came in thirty-first.

Born in 1947, Cheryl started running around her high school track after she read an article in the newspaper stating that jogging was a healthy way to lose weight. But a girl running around a track in full view of the boys? An official noticed and brought the matter to the board of education. The board ruled that her activities were inappropriate.

But Cheryl kept running. She joined the local Amateur Athletic Union track team, quickly realizing that she was naturally gifted at running distances. With the club, Cheryl earned national recognition in meets across the country. She went on to attend Indiana State

University, which—because it awarded scholarships to students with "special talents" (be it in academics or athletics)—gave Cheryl money to attend because of her running skill. That meant Cheryl effectively became the first woman in the United States to receive a collegiate athletic scholarship.

Still, the school didn't have a women's cross-country team, so Cheryl entered meets against high school boys. Officials allowed her to compete, so long as she gave the boys a five-second head start. She tried to be "ladylike" when she inevitably passed many of them.

Cheryl graduated college and moved to California. Inspired by the handful of women sneaking into marathons in Boston and elsewhere, Cheryl decided she wanted to finish the distance herself, which she did for the first time in 1970 with a time of three hours and fifteen minutes. But she wasn't done. She continued to train, logging sixty to seventy miles a week, and found a race that had softened its position on women competing—the Western Hemisphere Marathon, which was famous as the race where Merry Lepper had become the first North American woman to complete a marathon eight years earlier.

Cheryl began the race at a six-minute-and-six-second-per-mile pace. It felt easy. Until a man, not pleased that a woman was about to pass him in the race, tried to physically force her off the course. Other runners had to intervene. Cheryl sped away, finishing the race in 2:49:40. She became the first woman to break 2:50:00 in a marathon—and the new world record holder. Her name was now part of a lineage of record-breaking women just a few steps removed from Maureen's.

***

Women weren't just getting faster; more of them were competing in marathons.

Much of it had to do with Kathrine Switzer's anger. After she was nearly pulled off the course in Boston, she was banned from competition by the AAU. She ran a marathon with Maureen in Toronto and was thankful for Sy's invitation, but it didn't solve her problems back home.

Kathrine went on a mission to get women equal access to marathons and other long-distance running events. And her quest worked.

In 1972, the Boston Marathon officially opened up the race to women for the very first time. Kathrine placed third, running in 3:29:51. She then began working for the New York Road Runners, a new association with a charismatic leader named Fred Lebow, who supported Switzer's mission to spread distance-running equality.

By the fall of 1972, the American AAU ruled that women could officially participate in marathons. The catch: They had to start ten minutes after the men. The officials' logic was to maintain races that were "separate but equal."

This did not sit well with female runners, who staged a protest. At the starting line of the 1972 New York City Marathon, a 278-entrant race only in its third year, all six women running sat down in protest. Images of their act made it into papers around the globe, helping to force the AAU to change the rules and allow women to start at the same time as the men.

In 1977, a former-overweight-smoker-turned-runner named Jim Fixx published a book called *The Complete Book of Running*, which espoused the health benefits of running long distance, just for fun. It became a phenomenal bestseller, and a running craze swept the nation. Thousands of ordinary people laced up their shoes, put on sweatpants, and went outside to jog. They called it the first "Running Boom." Women, Switzer determined, shouldn't be left out of it.

The same year Fixx's book became a bestseller, Switzer founded the Avon International Running Circuit. Backed by one of the largest cosmetic companies in the world, the eight-race event—open only to women— traveled to seven cities around the United States. The final event took place in a small West Germany town called Waldniel, a location meant to honor a women's marathon pioneer named Dr. Ernst van Aaken.

Yes, the very same doctor who had encouraged his female athletes to run marathons to prove it was possible—all because of a thirteen-year-old girl from North York.

***

In 1984 the Olympics finally added a women's marathon to its lineup—eighty-eight years after men were first given the chance.

On a warm morning in early August, seventy-seven thousand people crammed inside the Los Angeles Memorial Coliseum to watch the finish of the marathon. When a lone figure, a woman in a gray singlet and white cap, emerged in full stride from a tunnel onto the maroon track, the stadium erupted. Joan Benoit (now Benoit Samuelson), a twenty-seven-year-old from Cape Elizabeth, Maine, sprinted one full lap in front of the largest crowd ever gathered to watch a women's distance event. Seventeen years after Maureen's world record, this former collegiate running star for tiny Bowdoin College earned the first gold medal in the women's marathon.

The race was broadcast live around the world, with

Kathrine Switzer helping commentate for the US network. In living rooms all around North America, little girls watched and dreamed. Here was proof that one day they, too, could hurtle into a packed stadium in a full, beautiful stride and earn an ovation from thousands.

Nineteen years later, in 2003, the British distance phenom Paula Radcliffe finished the London Marathon in 2:15:25—almost exactly an hour faster than Maureen. As of the fall of 2019, Paula's world record still stands, an irresistible target for competitive female runners all over the world.

Thankfully, women don't need a record anymore to prove their worth. Because millions have chosen to cover the distance, inspired by the running revolutionaries who came before them.

For forty years, Maureen Wilton had no idea she was one of those revolutionaries. Neither did the world.

25

There's a feeling journalists get when they know
they've discovered an amazing story. It's kind of like
an internal compass that, after jostling back and forth
for a moment, locks onto a heading. But whereas a
compass relies on the earth's magnetic field to point it
in the right direction, a radio documentary producer
named John Chipman needed only a skinny paragraph
on the back page of a small Canadian running magazine called *iRun*.

The publication was shoved inside a plastic bag next
to loose-leaf coupons, metal safety pins, and Chipman's
race bib for the 2009 Mississauga Marathon—a race of
1,400 people held in a town directly west of Toronto.
In his late thirties—lean from running regular weekly
miles with a face that usually bore stylish scruff—
Chipman was in the best shape of his life. Ahead of the
race, he was focused on running his personal best in
the marathon, hoping to break 3:10:00.

To pass the time, perhaps to distract himself from
the prerace jitters burbling in his stomach, Chipman began thumbing through the magazine until he

reached a section on the back page called the "iRun Index." In neatly printed paragraphs, the section listed notable running accomplishments achieved by Canadians. He recognized most of them. There was a description of Terry Fox—who, despite losing a leg to cancer, attempted to run the length of Canada in 1980 with a prosthetic limb, inspiring the nation to raise millions of dollars to help find a cure for the disease. There was Tom Longboat, a native Canadian from the Onondaga people, who won the Boston Marathon in 1907. As Chipman's eyes darted across the page from one legendary athlete to the next, he stopped on one name.

Maureen Wilton.

Chipman had been running for years and completed dozens of races. He was a die-hard fan of the sport. He'd recently started producing a running col umn for the Canadian Broadcasting Corporation, and he'd interviewed some of the most prominent Canadian distance runners of the past half century.

But he'd never seen the name Maureen Wilton before. Which is why what he read next shocked him.

In 1967, at the age of thirteen, this Toronto native set a world's best time for the women's marathon.

Questions began circling in Chipman's mind. How, being as plugged in to the running community as he was, had he never heard of this record or this girl? He knew that in the 1960s, women weren't encouraged or allowed to run long distances, so how did this girl pull it off? And more urgently, what happened to her? Where was she now?

If Chipman had a compass on him, it would have locked into place at that moment. He needed to find Maureen Wilton.

It wasn't easy.

Chipman finished the Mississauga Marathon on Sunday, May 10, in the fastest time of his life—3:08:59. Then he got to work, hunting for a key to a story that had taken place almost exactly forty-two years prior.

He started in the archives of the *Toronto Star* and the *Toronto Globe and Mail*. It wasn't hard to dig up old stories about the tiny preteen running sensation from North York who people called "Mighty Moe." Chipman learned about Sy Mah—a larger-than-life figure in Chipman's mind—who spearheaded a movement with his team of talented girls to advance equality in women's distance running.

Most stunning of all, Chipman read about Kathrine Switzer's appearance on the day the record fell, just two weeks after her own battle for equal running rights. It felt like he'd just dug up a time capsule that nobody knew existed. This was history the world had forgotten.

And the woman in the middle of it had not received the recognition she deserved.

For roughly two months, Chipman searched for a Maureen Wilton. He knew her last name could have changed if she'd married, which made the hunt that much more tricky.

His break came when he discovered a column in an old sports publication called *Athletics Magazine* from 1986. Over two pages, the article rehashed much of the information Chipman already knew. But one key paragraph said that Maureen had married a teacher named Paul Mancuso. Finally, Chipman had a lead. In a small notebook he carried in his pocket, he started writing down the name and phone number of every Mancuso who lived in the Toronto region. And he started calling them, crossing off names, one by one, if their calls came back with no new information.

In the summer of 2009, his phone finally rang displaying a strange number. He answered and heard a timid voice come through the receiver.

"This is Maureen," the voice said.

***

The phone call from a random journalist shocked Maureen, because for years she'd kept her success a secret—even from her daughter. When Carolyn Mancuso came home from elementary school with a permission slip to participate in cross country, Maureen responded, "Now, why on earth would you want to do that? Do you know how much work it's going to be?"

"I get a day off from school for the race," said Carolyn. "Can you just sign the permission slip, please?"

Maureen did. And that spring, she drove Carolyn to school an hour early every day to train with other grade-three-through-six kids on the team. They'd stretch in the gym and then run a loop around the small track and baseball diamond.

Although her mom dropped her off every morning, Carolyn prohibited Maureen from watching. Maybe it was because of her mom's reaction to the permission slip. Or maybe it was because, from a young age, Carolyn liked to do things alone. But Carolyn couldn't stop her mother from sneaking a peek now and then.

What Maureen saw, crouching behind their family car to spy on the practices, was Carolyn picking daisies. Sure, she ran for the first leg or two, but by the upper yard, she was strolling... then stopping. To. Pick. Flowers.

Seriously? We're getting up an hour early each day for this?

But Maureen kept delivering her daughter to the morning practices.

And later that spring, the end-of-season meet was held at a park not far from Carolyn's elementary school. Teams from different schools gathered at the starting area, pitching tents and keeping warm under blankets. Carolyn was one of seventy-seven girls from grades three and four to compete in the two-kilometer race that day. She had butterflies as they gathered at the starting line, not because she wanted to win exactly, but because she wanted to do well and there were a lot of people watching.

When the air horn blasted, Carolyn took off in a tangle of arms and legs. The crowd of runners turned right, past a giant monument, along the edge of the park, up the bunny slope of a small ski area, past some trees, and into the final straightaway to the finish line. Or at least that's what most runners did. Carolyn ran out of power almost immediately, oblivious to the other runners flying by her.

Maureen watched as her daughter finished second to last.

Carolyn certainly didn't inherit any running talent, Maureen couldn't help thinking. But she kept her thoughts to herself.

The next year, Carolyn joined the team again. This time around, she decided to try a little harder in practice—just a little. She started by picking checkpoints when she was tired, promising herself that she wouldn't walk until she reached a certain tree. And then she picked another point where she'd start running again. She let the flowers be.

At the meet that year, Carolyn settled at the starting line of the 1500-meter race, fighting off the familiar nervous stomach. There were faster runners, but perhaps she could come in more toward the middle of the pack?

"How many flowers do you think Carolyn will pick this race?" Maureen asked her own mother, who'd come to cheer on her granddaughter.

"Oh, stop it," said Margaret, pressing PLAY on the video recorder to catch the start of the race.

The air horn blasted; the girls took off. After the runners disappeared from view, Maureen and her mother followed the other spectators to the final stretch to await the racers.

When the first runners reached the final cluster of trees, Carolyn's two-person cheering squad couldn't believe what they saw.

Carolyn was up front with the leaders, shoulder to shoulder with a taller runner, chased by dozens. There were only two other runners in front of her. She had a very real shot at third place.

"Look . . . look at that stride!" Carolyn's grandmother said to Maureen. "It looks like I am watching you run again."

Maureen didn't respond. She was watching her daughter in awe. Carolyn's arms pumped like pistons, and her long stride seemed impossible for someone with such a small frame.

As her daughter passed in front of them, a half roar, half yell escaped from Maureen: "Go, go, go!"

A startled Carolyn looked over at her mom and then took off like a rocket, beating her nearest competitor to the finish to capture third place.

The award's effect on the fourth grader was instantaneous: *She was a runner.* She knew it in her bones. Her transformation from flower picker to medal winner was so sudden, it almost felt like she'd had this switch inside her the whole time. She just needed the third place finish to flip it on.

That evening they gathered to celebrate Carolyn's achievement—her mom and dad, her younger brother, her grandmother and grandfather, who was still alive then. While clearing the table with her grandmother after dinner, Carolyn was turning the events over in her head: her third-place finish, the feeling that she could have kept running forever, her desire to do it again and again. And then, out of the blue, one clear question came to her.

"Grandma, did my mom ever run?"

***

The urge to run never fully left Maureen's body. It just got buried by the passage of time, by school and jobs, by nurturing two kids, by tragedy, like the death of both her brothers.

But under each new layer of her life—both the gloriously happy and the terribly sad—remained that incessant little desire to *feel fast*. Her daughter, Carolyn, had been running for her local track club the past few years, and Maureen loved almost nothing more than watching her offspring fall in love with the same sport that had defined Maureen's life at nearly the exact same age. But that's all Maureen did—watch. What changed on a bitter winter day in 2003? She is not sure. But all of a sudden, she didn't want to sit in the bleachers anymore. She wanted to run.

She laced up her shoes and drove with Carolyn to a nearby indoor track-and-field facility. Together, on a red oval with rubberized surface (cinder tracks were old-school), they sprinted through eight 200-meter repeats. Carolyn darted in front as Maureen let her feet and legs remember the thrilling, repetitive thrum of a sprinting stride. They both gasped for air at the end of each sprint. Maureen knew that feeling. It was lungs-chugging, abdomen-tightening, arms-swinging freedom. Oh, how she missed it. She wanted more.

Maureen didn't consider the significance of the moment. She didn't connect its location—a new building on the campus of York University—to the start line of her record-breaking marathon, which had happened mere feet away almost four decades earlier. She didn't notice that when they ran together, her daughter was thirteen years old, the same age as Maureen when she broke the record.

Instead, Maureen reveled in the movement. To her great surprise, she could still run at fifty years old. But more than that, she still loved to run. And for the next five years, she'd satiate that urge whenever she got the chance. She went out with Carolyn to the track or ran around her neighborhood. Not once did she have the desire to race, though. She didn't need that pressure.

What she didn't know was that racing had changed. She'd been gone from the sport so long that she had no idea that millions of people now signed up for races just for the pleasure of being out on the road with other people, for the joy of the personal challenge. Most of the people who signed up for races had very little interest in winning. Without this knowledge, Maureen remained in her own isolated world, running just to run—running just to feel fast again.

But something was missing.

The passing decades allowed Maureen to think about and process her time on the North York Track Club. She still didn't believe her marathon on May 6, 1967, would ever mean that much, but she did come to realize that the most important part of her running career—the reason she loved it most—was the community of people who shared in the accomplishments. It wasn't the competition that kept her coming back to the Earl Haig cinder track on weeknights after school. It was the other runners and parents and coaches. Now, as an adult and a mother of two, she set out to find that community again.

The Longboat Roadrunners, named after legendary Canadian distance runner and Boston Marathon champ Tom Longboat, met every Saturday in High Park at eight A.M. Founded in 1980, the club hosted more than a hundred members. On a warm morning in June 2009, Maureen drove twenty minutes to a parking lot in front of a restaurant on the edge of the park—the same one she had raced in almost a half century before.

She turned off the ignition and looked around to see a group of men and women in brightly colored performance gear stretching and chatting. She felt shy, nervous about introducing herself to a new group of people. She was surprised there were so many of them. Forty-six years ago, her mom made her hop out of the car and tell a stranger she wanted to run. Now, alone, she did the exact same thing. She approached the group with a small smile.

"Hi," she said. "My name is Maureen. Can I run with you?"

26

"I found her," John Chipman said excitedly into the phone. Kathrine Switzer was on the other end of the line. "She wants to get in contact with you."

It was July 2009, and Chipman was finally orchestrating a reunion decades in the making. His aim was to produce a radio documentary on the CBC about two running pioneers: one who had become world-famous, and one who was never recognized by the world.

Kathrine couldn't believe Chipman was able to track down the speedy little girl who'd been obsessed with the Monkees. She'd always wondered what had happened to Maureen. She suspected that, because Maureen had started at such a young age, she'd eventually burn out and quit.

Switzer was right, in a way. But she had no idea just how completely Maureen had shut herself off from the sport or how thoroughly she'd buried her time in the club, speaking to almost no one about it for decades.

In a famous short story published in 1819 by Washington Irving, a character named Rip Van Winkle falls asleep for twenty years while hunting in the Catskill

Mountains and snores through the American Revolution. He wakes up to find a world that's completely transformed.

When Kathrine and Maureen reconnected, Maureen reminded Kathrine of Van Winkle. Maureen had quit running when women simply didn't run marathons because it was like "pushing peanuts up a hill"—a meaningless act that would amount to nothing, said critics. If they did run marathons, outside of a small group of supporters, they were treated with disapproval, if not outright scorn. It was as if Maureen had fallen asleep in 1969 and completely missed another revolution, one that allowed and celebrated the millions of women who crossed finish lines around the world.

It wasn't enough for Kathrine to appear on a radio documentary with Maureen. She and Chipman invited Maureen to run the Goodlife Fitness Toronto Half Marathon. As a leader of a running revolution, Kathrine decided it was about time to wake up one of the people who'd helped start it.

***

Why is this marathon such a big deal? Maureen wondered. She was flattered when a journalist called wanting her to share her story, but she was sure few would care. She didn't mention her past to coworkers.

She didn't mention it to her new friends in the Longboat Roadrunners, either. For all they knew, when she arrived to the park each Saturday in July, August, and September 2009, she was there as one of many who had been swept up by the women's running boom. An exceptionally talented runner, yes, but one who'd joined the sport to have some fun and stay healthy.

When John Chipman and Kathrine Switzer asked her to register for the half marathon, she agreed mostly out of curiosity. She wanted to see if races had changed at all. She also wanted to see if she could still run fast, pass people with purpose, and feel the thrilling pain of a final push to the finish line, even at the age of fifty-five.

The evening before the race, Switzer was scheduled to give a motivational talk to runners. This speech, in a ballroom over dinner, was one of the dozens that she gives each year at running events around the world. Roughly a hundred people sat around circular tables eating the last bites of their meal as she took the stage. Like a politician running for office, Kathrine had prepared remarks that she typically gives at these events. They focus on the event that she's most famous for: the Boston Marathon in 1967. She usually covers that historic race, how it felt to be targeted by a race director simply for being a woman, and how it powered her quest for women's equality in running going forward.

She talks about her win in the New York City Marathon in 1974 and her successful push to make the women's marathon an Olympic event.

But that night, she looked down at Maureen, sitting at one of the tables in front of a finished plate of pasta, and decided to toss aside her standard statements.

"I'd like to share a story about running's own Rip Van Winkle," Switzer began. The room fell silent as Switzer recounted her experience running a thirty-person race on a dusty road in a rural suburb of Toronto many, many years ago. She went on to describe meeting a wispy little girl who ran the race, too, finishing more than an hour ahead of her.

She talked about the world record the girl broke that day and the lackluster reaction it received. She talked about how, on the car ride home from the race, she and her friends predicted the girl would quit. She talked about the disappearance of the girl, and how, over the past forty years, running flourished. She finished the speech by looking straight at Maureen.

"That girl is with us here tonight," Switzer said. "Her name is Maureen Wilton Mancuso."

The room erupted into applause as Switzer encouraged Maureen to stand up. The noise may as well have been as loud as a stadium ovation—overwhelming applause and recognition that came decades too late.

Maureen smiled wide. This, she realized, was her moment.

***

But she still had a race to finish.

Everything about the 2009 Goodlife Fitness Toronto Half Marathon differed from any race Maureen had run in the past. For starters, whole blocks in the heart of the city were cordoned off. No rural roads on the outskirts of town this time around.

She also worried about her mom, who was now eighty-four years old. The start was going to be frigid and dark. And how was Margaret going to reach the finish line with Maureen's bag of warm clothes?

Kathrine had to laugh when Maureen laid out her concerns. More than 8,000 people were going to run this race. Kathrine told Maureen that Margaret wouldn't be able to get anywhere near the start or finish line to spectate. But that was okay! Fortunately, in the forty years since Maureen had left running, race management had advanced, too. Participants could now hand off their postrace gear in marked bags, which would then be hauled off in trucks and delivered to the finish line.

Maureen was also befuddled by a plastic orange band that came with her bib. Kathrine had to explain that it was a timing chip, which you're supposed to attach to your shoe. The band included a sensor that records a runner's time along the course.

And now Maureen had to laugh. At least there was no chance that a faulty blue Bulova watch would cause her to panic before the finish.

Maureen was ready. Her extra clothes were on their way to the finish line. Her timing chip was on her shoe. There were runners everywhere, shaking out their arms and legs, stretching. When the race finally started, *the sound!* Maureen was astounded. She could hear other runners' footsteps. So many footsteps. As thousands of rubber soles pattered against the asphalt, it sounded like a rainstorm. The noise overwhelmed Maureen. In all her years of running, she'd never run with so many people. She'd never heard anything like that sound before.

For five years in the 1960s, Maureen Wilton had been a runner. It defined her life. It dictated what she ate and how she dressed, the people she hung out with, and the places she visited. She found her best friends through running. Running changed her life and her parents' lives. And for all the work she put in, Maureen became the best in the world. But the best in the world at a distance that women weren't allowed to run. The pressure of that position, the nonstop training, the criticism, friends moving, getting injured, quitting. It stopped feeling worth it. It didn't seem to matter enough to sacrifice her happiness. So Maureen quit.

But this roaring shower of footsteps on a clean asphalt road in the center of the city she called home? It signified just how many people *did* care.

Maureen left running in part because the community that encouraged her to do it crumbled. But it was a community she'd never forget.

Sy Mah moved away and became an assistant professor of Health Promotion and Human Performance at the University of Toledo until his death in 1988. After running his first marathon with Maureen in 1967, he went on to run 523 more. He held, at one time, the world record for the most marathons ever finished by one person.

Sheila Meharg, after setting a three-mile Canadian record that would last for decades, quit to pursue interests in art and music. She traveled, lived on Canada's east and west coasts. She got married and raised three boys. Today, she gets her music fix by singing with the worship team at her church.

Carol Haddrall got a degree in chemistry and a secondary degree in science. She picked up tennis, got married, and had two boys. She was a teacher for more than thirty years. She went back to school in her sixties to get a psychology degree.

Jo-Ann Rowe healed from her spinal fusion surgery. Six months later, she returned to sports, this time as an instructor of swimming, alpine skiing, and waterskiing. She became a nurse, eventually overseeing more than 1,000 nurses. She also opened her own nurse education business.

The North York Track Club itself disbanded in the 1970s as other running clubs formed in the area and attracted away talent.

But Maureen's world record and all her other myriad accomplishments rippled far beyond the people in the club she knew best. Her records traveled to Germany and New York City. The rebellion she began continued on starting lines and with race directors all over the country and even on the Olympic stage. And then, in events directly connected to her, marathon running for women broke wide. Here, on the Toronto streets, these thousands and thousands of runners were part of a new community ready to welcome back Maureen, the woman in some way responsible for getting them to the starting line in the first place.

At mile nine of the 13.1-mile race, Maureen ran up next to a buff man in a black T-shirt and a white baseball cap. She could hear his labored breathing and she noticed how he slunk forward with arms that swayed too far. He looked like he was struggling.

Maureen settled in next to him and they began to chat. Perhaps forty years earlier she would have sped up, passed him to grab a higher position in the finishing ranks. Instead, she stayed with him. She encouraged him. She cajoled him (with a smile) into maintaining his pace.

The man noticed her smooth stride, how she looked like she was floating over the asphalt. Between breaths, he sputtered out a question. "Have you done one of these before?"

Maureen smiled.

"Yeah, I did a marathon once," she said. "But that was a long time ago."

26.2

The girl is supposed to be here.

The girl—now a woman—is standing on the left side of a paved road, at the front of an idling parade of humanity. Behind her, fifty thousand people are anxious to start moving. They form a nearly mile-long caravan that, in a few moments, will start streaming forward for 26.2 miles through the charming brownstones, industrial factories, and glistening skyscrapers of New York City.

Many of the fifty thousand have never done this before—run a marathon. They shed their nerves by chatting with neighbors, laughing, or taking final sips of water. They'll be thrilled to simply finish. Others have run four, five, or even a dozen races just like this. They have a time in mind—a race strategy they've been plotting for months. They'll be happy if they can run faster than they have before. Only a tiny cluster at the front of the mass, women and men in brightly colored, skintight racing singlets, carry the singular and seemingly impossible goal to win.

The girl is among them.

She is wearing a fire-engine-red-and-jet-black racing singlet. On each arm, from the wrist up to her shoulder, she's also wearing sleeves—one red and one black—to keep her warm. It's cloudy and a chilly fifty-six degrees on this November morning in 2017. A slight breeze rustles her gleaming blond hair, which is up in a ponytail and held back by a skinny red headband.

Flashes of neon yellow, pink, orange, and blue ripple through the group of women as they jump and flex and warm up their sculpted muscles. They all jiggle their arms and legs to their own rhythm. Some peek at watches strapped around their wrists. Others gaze straight ahead, down the open expanse of pavement. They're standing, toes pointed straight ahead, behind a blue-and-orange mat stretched across the entire road. Their faces look hardened, serious. Their muscles tense.

A few feet in front of them, a motorcycle idles next to a small cavalry of police cars emitting a soft rumbling. Sitting backward on the seat, a man with a video camera points his lens at the group, broadcasting the scene to millions around the world.

A booming voice echoes out of speakers lined along the road so everyone in the massive crowd can hear.

"On your marks."

The girl is familiar with the silence that follows—the

few seconds when the globe feels like it's stopped rotating and nothing seems to matter except for a ferocious will to move forward on two feet as fast as possible.

The girl leans.

A cannon fires, ejecting a stream of smoke. The girl, among a herd of the fastest female marathoners in the world, dashes through the white haze.

For 364 days a year, the bridges, avenues, streets, and blocks that are stitched together to form the New York City Marathon course rumble and screech as taxicabs, cars, bicycles, and trucks trundle their way through the chaos. But on the first Sunday of each November, the traffic clears. More than a million people stand behind cold metal barricades or on sidewalks or behind windows in buildings high above the action, waiting to catch a brief glimpse of the runners, in their full, beautiful stride, battling to reach the finish line in the heart of Manhattan—Central Park.

As the spectators gather, they check their phones or chat with their neighbors. A question ripples up and down the sidewalks.

Where is the girl?

Of the fifty thousand runners, she is the one the spectators most want to see win. She would be the first American to win the race since 1977. They scream her name as she streaks by, cupping their hands over their mouths, as if their small burst of energy will help push her forward.

But the girl isn't ready to lead yet. She's biding her time. She moves in the pack like she's a fish in a large school, mimicking the movements of those in front of and around her. When one pushes ahead, trying to create space, she follows.

The pack of women glides through the raucous crowds in Brooklyn, through wide avenues in Queens, and over the intertwining gray steel of the Queensboro Bridge. Coming off the ramp leading to First Avenue in Manhattan, they reach the section called Thunder Alley, named for the deafening screams of thousands of fans. One by one, women fade from the lead group. The girl doesn't. She runs on the right side of the road, a shoulder-length behind the front-runner.

Her movement is hypnotic, peaceful even. Her head bobs up and down in an even rhythm in a way that would seem relaxing until you see how shockingly fast the white traffic paint on the road flashes by her feet. Her pace is steady at nearly five minutes and thirty seconds per mile.

By mile twenty, only three women remain in the front pack, including the girl.

Six miles away on metal bleachers next to the finish line, a growing crowd of people glue their eyes to a massive screen, displayed in front of the trees in Central Park. An unspoken energy starts to burble among the spectators. They're beginning to believe this American girl can win a race that has been dominated for three decades by amazing runners from Europe, Africa, and Mexico.

At mile twenty-two, so does the girl. She takes the lead, trailed by two women. The group is less a cluster now and more a string. Like taffy, it stretches as the girl pulses forward.

The crowd's belief in her is growing. They scream louder. The girl speeds up.

At mile twenty-five, she is alone, soaring forward. Her blond ponytail bounces with every powerful step. On the massive screen by the finish line, her image is projected nearly three times larger than she is in real life. She is the center of attention for everyone in the stands and the millions of others watching her race around the world.

You can see the moment the girl knows she is going to win. Her face morphs from steely focus to unbridled happiness. In full stride, just a hundred meters from the finish line, she starts to cry. She raises her fist in the air. "Yes!" she screams.

The crowd screams right back. Women all over the country, leaning toward their televisions, cry at the sight of her, too.

With her arms raised above her ponytail, tears streaming down her face, the girl breaks through tape held by two volunteers under a blue arch. An American flag is draped around her shoulders.

The girl's name is Shalane Flanagan. She's just won the biggest marathon in the world. In a few minutes, she'll stand atop a podium and be presented with a check for $100,000. In a few weeks she'll star in a Nike commercial. In a few months, little girls across the country will tie their hair into a ponytail, don a fire-engine-red-and-jet-black singlet, and dress up like their idol for Halloween.

But right now, in the frenetic seconds after fulfilling her dreams, she lets the roar of the crowd splash over her. She knows she is supposed to be here.

Why? Because more than twenty years ago she laced up running shoes and discovered the sheer, satisfying joy of moving forward. She was encouraged to do so by her mother, a woman named Cheryl Bridges, who, more than twenty years before that—in 1971—broke a marathon world record. A record able to be broken because four years before that, a thirteen-year-old girl ran a marathon with twenty-eight men on a dusty road in Toronto. Technically, Maureen Wilton wasn't supposed to be there.

But she ran anyway.

AFTERWORD
Des Linden

At 6:30 A.M. on April 16, 2018—about six months after my friend and rival Shalane's victory in New York City—the Boston Marathon's John Hancock Elite Athlete Field exited the Fairmont Copley Plaza Hotel to board the waiting charter buses. When the hotel door swung open one thing was very obvious: on this day conditions would play a major factor in the race outcome. Outside the temperature was just above freezing, there were torrential downpours and winds of fifteen to twenty miles per hour with gusts up to forty-five miles per hour. The assembled media in the press room had already suggested it was the worst weather in the 122-year history of the Boston Marathon.

The mood on the athlete bus was beyond tense as we followed our police escort out to the race starting line in Hopkinton. It didn't settle when we entered the Korean church where the elite athletes are kept warm and dry before the race gets underway. And it certainly never eased as we lined up on the start line and prepared to contest the most historic marathon in the world.

At the crack of the starter's pistol, forty-eight elite

women headed out into the conditions first and led the way for the rest of the 30,000 runners. We followed behind the designated women's press truck that broadcasted our story to the world. The 2018 race was filled with incredible runners from around the globe: Olympians, World Marathon Major winners, and some of the fastest runners of all time.

When you ask professional runners, "What draws you to Boston?" both the history and the tradition are a part of every athlete's answer. Every professional runner is aware of the many epic battles that have unfolded on the roads from Hopkinton to Boston over the hundred-plus years of racing on the route. They know Boston can make you a legend like American heroes Bill Rodgers and Joan Benoit, or four-time champion Catherine Ndereba of Kenya, also known as "Catherine the Great." In the 2018 edition we covered the same hallowed ground as our heroes and the thousands of others that have made the trek over those storied 26.2 miles. We just had a little extra rain and wind to contend with.

Two hours and thirty-nine minutes after the starting gun went off, I found myself breaking the finishing tape on Boylston and running myself into the Boston history books. It was life-changing. The media storm that followed would focus on me being the first

American winner in thirty-three years, ending the American drought, and doing it all in what was largely considered the most difficult conditions in Boston Marathon history. I would have to respectfully disagree with the last assertion. It was the most difficult conditions in men's Boston Marathon history. The women pushed through the conditions knowing we could handle them and so much more, because the most difficult conditions in women's marathon history were battled by the likes of Bobbi Gibb, Kathrine Switzer, and Maureen Wilton. The rain, wind, and freezing temperatures paled in comparison to the battles waged by the trailblazers before us. In their fight to give women an opportunity in our sport, our heroes taught us that we can handle so much more than anyone thought possible.

SOURCES

Author Interviews

Over the course of a year we spoke with more than a dozen people, with our tape recorders on, either in person or by phone. Their memories, most significantly Maureen (Wilton) Mancuso's, served as the largest source of information for the book. Other interview subjects included Roberta (Picco) Angeloni, Jacki (Ford) Bisborrow, Lynne Borque, John Chipman, Carol (Haddrall) Fawcett, Sheila (Meharg) MacDonald, Rico Madero, Carolyn Mancuso, Paul Mancuso, Bob Moore, John Reeves, Jo-Ann Rowe, Doug Smith, Kathrine Switzer, and Margaret Wilton.

Newspapers

This book, quite simply, wouldn't be possible without a collection of four scrapbooks, meticulously curated by Margaret Wilton over Maureen's time as a runner. The collection includes hundreds of clippings, spanning from 1963 to 1969. They offer a vivid portrait of Sy Mah's media savvy, the growth of the North York Track Club, the controversy around Maureen's marathon, and her success as a long-distance runner. Margaret often cut out only the sections mentioning her daughter, leaving out the author, name of the newspaper, and date of publication. Nevertheless, we were able to deduce the rough dates based on the articles' placement in the scrapbook, reporting from other papers, Maureen's own memory, and her extensive trophy collection. The articles were sourced from a wide range of local Toronto papers, including the *Mirror*, *Globe and Mail*, *Star*, and a few local North York publications that no longer exist.

Video and Audio

We started this project because of two audio projects. First, John Chipman's phenomenal radio documentary "Did My Mom Ever Run?" which aired in 2009 on the Canadian Broadcasting Corporation, reuniting Maureen and Kathrine Switzer for the first time in over forty years (www.cbc.ca/sportslongform/entry/how-a-13-year-old-canadian-girl-ran-the-worlds-fastest-marathon). Second, a 2017 episode we wrote and produced for the *Runner's World* podcast *Human Race*. The episode is entitled "Little Moe" (www.runnersworld.com/runners-stories/a20853804/episode-19-little-mo).

While no video footage exists of Moe's world-record marathon, we were able to watch eight-millimeter footage of both a race and a practice to see what she looked like in full stride (hint: it's fast). As part of our research, we also had the pleasure of rewatching footage of the women's 100-meter and 800-meter races at the 1928 Olympics, Abebe Bikila's 1964 world record marathon, Paula Radcliffe's record race in 2003, and Shalane Flanagan's incredible win at the 2017 New York City Marathon—all of which you can watch on YouTube.

Books

We consulted many books during our research that highlight and celebrate the achievements of women's running pioneers. Below is a list of the sources we relied on most. For young readers looking for more information about inspiring runners from Maureen's time period (or even earlier), we recommend starting with Amby Burfoot's *First Ladies of Running* and Kathrine Switzer's *Marathon Woman* (which does explore some adult themes).

Burfoot, Amby. *First Ladies of Running: 22 Inspiring Profiles of the Rebels, Rule Breakers, and Visionaries Who Changed the Sport Forever*. New York: Rodale, 2016.

Hanc, John. *The B.A.A. at 125: The Official History of the Boston Athletic Association, 1887–2012*. Boston: Sports Publishing, 2012.

Humber, Charles J., ed. *Canada: From Sea Unto Sea*. Mississauga, ON: The Loyalist Press Limited, 1986.

Martin, David E. and Roger W. H. Gynn. *The Olympic Marathon: The History and Drama of Sport's Most Challenging Event*. Champaign, IL: Human Kinetics, 2000.

Montillo, Roseanne. *Fire on the Track: Betty Robinson and the Triumph of the Early Olympic Women*. New York: Crown, 2017.

Mossman, Gary. *Lloyd Percival: Coach and Visionary*. Woodstock, ON: Seraphim Editions, 2013.

Switzer, Kathrine. *Marathon Woman: Running the Race to Revolutionize Women's Sports*. Boston: Da Capo Press, 2009.

Magazines and Periodicals

Cinderbelle: News and Views of Women's Track and Field. Ohio Hall of Fame track coach Steve Price loaned us six issues of this newsletter, which spanned from September 1966 to May 1967. It provides an incredible window into the growth of women's track and distance running. More incredible was the fact that it even existed. In a time when women struggled to gain equality on the track and roads, this wonderful publication served as a resource and inspiration for the thousands of girls who wanted to run anyway.

Blaikie, David. "Mighty Mo." *Athletics: Canada's National Track and Field/Running Magazine*, June 1986. 44–45. This was the first retrospective article to mention Maureen as a running pioneer.

Rogin, Gilbert. "Flamin' Mamie's Bouffant Belles." *Sports Illustrated*, April 20, 1964. This article offers interesting, if infuriating, insight into how women track-and-field athletes were viewed in the era. The cover of this issue served as the first time women's track athletes were featured so prominently in the magazine's history.

Switzer, Kathrine. "Rip Van Winkle Awakens in Toronto." *Marathon and Beyond*, May/June 2011. 16–22. After reuniting with Maureen in 2009, Kathrine Switzer wrote this article, which details her surreal experience reintroducing Maureen back into the (now booming) running world.

NOTES

Part I

Details about Maureen's life were provided by Maureen and her mother, Margaret, and supplemented by Wilton family photo albums. Newspaper articles in Maureen's scrapbooks, assembled by her mother, helped us understand how the club grew and the details of individual races. In interviews, Maureen and her teammates Carol (Haddrall) Fawcett, Sheila (Meharg) MacDonald, and Jo-Ann Rowe provided additional details about Sy, the club, and club-related events.

Chapter 3

Details of the Olympic history, including the quotations from newspapers about the reactions to the first women's races, from Montillo, *Fire on the Track*, 78–84.

Descriptions of American Betty Robinson winning the first women's 100-meter Olympic gold medal come from video footage of the race posted on YouTube.

29 "The most efficient way": Joseph Levy, Danny Rosenberg and Avi Hyman, "Fanny "Bobbie" Rosenfeld: Canada's Woman Athlete of the Half Century," *Journal of Sport History*, Vol. 26, No. 2 (Summer 1999), pp. 392–96.

32 "There are two ways": Sarah Barker, "Why the 800 Comes Down to Hunters and the Hunted," *Deadspin*, April 24, 2015, www.deadspin.com/why-the-800-comes-down-to-hunters-and-the-hunted-1699308516.

Chapter 5

The main descriptions of Brenda's beginnings in the sport come from a magazine article from Margaret Wilton's scrapbook (David Blaikie, "Mighty Mo," *Athletics*) and a newspaper piece published just prior to her start in the club (*Toronto Globe and Mail*, "Boo Officials, Then Cheer as Girl Competes," March 27, 1964).

Author interviews, scrapbook articles, and published photos helped paint a picture in chapters six and seven of the club when Maureen and Brenda were the only members.

Chapter 6

58 "During one journalist's visit": Jack Marks, "Future Olympic Medals," *Toronto Globe and Mail.*

Description of the day when Maureen ran two races that were two hours apart and in two different cities came from detailed accounts in scrapbooks, including one, author and publication unknown, titled "Old Iron Man Act Is Done by Girls 10 and 11."

Chapter 7

64 "I don't think it's healthy for children": Jack Marks, "Future Olympic Medals."

65 "hasn't missed a day of school in two years": Jack Marks, "Future Olympic Medals."

65 "She used to eat like a bird": Jack Marks, "Future Olympic Medals."

Details and quotations about the race in New York come from a scrapbook article titled "Local Girls Steal Show in U.S. Run," author, publication, and date unknown.

Chapter 8

74 "You hear about troubles with the younger generation": Scrapbook article titled "Mayor Lauds Racers," author, publication, and date unknown.

Chapter 10

Information on Lloyd Percival drawn from Mossman, *Lloyd Percival,* and from an interview with Roberta (Picco) Angeloni.

Chapter 11

Excerpts and information about the growth of women's track come from issues of *Cinderbelle: News and Views of Women's Track and Field.*

Quotations from Dick Beyst and stories about the Lincoln Park Parkettes come from an author interview with Jacki (Ford) Bisborrow.

108 "its athletic achievements": Rogin, "Flamin' Mamie's Bouffant Belles."

Chapter 12

118 "Did that little girl win?": Scrapbook article titled "Maureen Wilton Pushes Picco to Close Finish," author, publication, and date unknown.

Part II

Most of the information in this section, in particular details about the Eastern Canadian Marathon Centennial Championships, came from author interviews with Maureen (Wilton) Mancuso, Margaret Wilton, Kathrine Switzer, and John Reeves—one of the only living men who raced in the marathon that day. Details about Kathrine Switzer's experience leading up to and during the Boston Marathon are sourced from her memoir, *Marathon Woman*.

Chapter 13

Details of the legend of Pheidippides drawn from Martin and Gynn, *The Olympic Marathon*, 1–23.

129 "impractical, uninteresting, ungainly": Jules Boykoff, "How Women Overcame More Than 100 Years of Olympic Controversy to Take Centre Stage at Rio," *Telegraph*, August 5, 2016.

129 "women should not exercise as men do": Author unknown, "Advises Women Not to Overdo in Exercising," *Detroit Free Press*, May 29, 1931.

129 "Pretty soon they have a beard": James Aswell, "My New York," *Hammond Times*, May 19, 1936.

Chapter 14

Details on Merry Lepper running the Western Hemisphere Marathon from Burfoot, *First Ladies of Running*, 33–42.

138 *"If the girls run"*: Scrapbook article titled "Mah vs. AAU Over Marathon," author and publication unknown, c. April 1967.

Chapter 15

141 *"The real game is on the field"*: Switzer, *Marathon Woman*, 9.

144 *"Oh, Arnie, let's quit talking"*: Switzer, *Marathon Woman*, 48.

History of the Boston Athletic Association comes from Hanc, *The B.A.A. at 125*, 23–42.

150 *"Get the hell out of my race"*: Switzer, *Marathon Woman*, 91.

Chapter 16

157 *"I know the AAU is not anxious"*: Personal note from Sy Mah to Kathrine Switzer, April 23, 1967.

Chapter 17

Names of competitors and course information come from the official race program and course map in Margaret Wilton's scrapbooks.

171 *"Why do all these people"*: Sy Mah's personal written account of the marathon, May 1967.

Part III

The finish line scene and aftermath of the Eastern Canadian Marathon Centennial Championships are based on author interviews with Maureen (Wilton) Mancuso, Margaret Wilton, and Kathrine Switzer, plus dozens of newspaper articles kept in Margaret's scrapbook collection.

Chapter 18

Details of Abebe Bikila's win at the 1964 Olympic Marathon in Tokyo from Martin and Gynn, *The Olympic Marathon*, 241–256.

Details of Bikila's finish are drawn from original footage of the race on YouTube.

Results from the race, including Maureen's time of 3:15:22.8, documented in multiple scrapbook articles.

189 "Moe made it in three fifteen": Sy Mah's personal account of the marathon, May 1967.

189 "Perhaps the most astounding moment": Sy Mah's personal account of the marathon, May 1967.

190 "slow runner but truly phenomenal": Scrapbook article titled "Run, Baby, Run," author, publication, and date unknown.

191 "We understand Maureen Wilton is only thirteen": Scrapbook article titled "It's Important That She Cares," author unknown, *Mirror*, May 10, 1967.

191 "Toronto Girl, 13, Sets World Mark": "It's Important That She Cares," *Mirror*.

192 "was like pushing peanuts up a hill with your nose": "It's Important That She Cares," *Mirror*.

192 "nothing special in Wilton's time": Scrapbook article, title, author, publication, and date unknown.

193 "Let's face it, no words": "It's Important That She Cares," *Mirror*.

194 "Five runners have finished": The entire poem is preserved in Maureen's scrapbook.

Chapter 19

Information drawn from scrapbook articles and author interviews with Maureen (Wilton) Mancuso, Margaret Wilton, and Paul Mancuso.

Chapter 20

Author interviews with Maureen (Wilton) Mancuso, Margaret Wilton, Jo-Ann Rowe, Sheila (Meharg) MacDonald, and Carol (Haddrall) Fawcett. We also consulted scrapbook articles about the Police Games Marathon.

Chapter 21

Author interviews with Maureen (Wilton) Mancuso, Carol (Haddrall) Fawcett, Margaret Wilton, Jo-Ann Rowe, and Sheila (Meharg) MacDonald.

Information about Sy's departure come from interviews plus selected articles, the most descriptive of which is a scrapbook article by Jon Penner, "Track Coach Sy Mah Quits," publication and date unknown.

Information about Peter Mason's appointment comes from a scrapbook article by Clare Butler, "Peter Mason Appointed Head Coach N.Y.T.C.," date and publication unknown.

Chapter 22

Maureen's personal photo albums, Scotland program, and news articles sourced from author interviews with Maureen (Wilton) Mancuso, Jo-Ann Rowe, and Roberta Angeloni.

Chapter 23

Author interviews with Maureen (Wilton) Mancuso and Margaret Wilton.

239 "I feel kind of badly about it": David Blaikie, "Mighty Mo," *Athletics*, June 1986, 44–45.

Chapter 24

244 "Run many miles": Ernst van Aaken, *Van Aaken Method*. Mountain View, California: World Publications, 1976.

Information about Anni Pede and Cheryl Bridges comes from Burfoot's *First Ladies of Running*. Information about Switzer comes from her memoir, *Marathon Woman*.

Chapter 26.2

Descriptions of the 2017 New York City Marathon come from footage of the race, aired on November 4 on ESPN, various clips now available on YouTube.

ACKNOWLEDGMENTS

We are thankful to so many people who shared their stories, personal archives, and connections with us in the course of reporting this story. But this project would not have been possible without Moe, who spent endless hours with us recounting her memories and schlepping us through Toronto on a tour of her childhood haunts. Her generosity, patience, and enthusiasm powered this project. And her drive, kindness, and bravery inspired it.

We are so grateful to Moe's mother, Margaret Wilton, who not only didn't say "no" or "you can't" when her only daughter came asking to run, but had the foresight to keep hundreds and hundreds of newspaper clippings about Maureen's running life. Without them, and her clarifying conversations, this book would not be possible.

Thanks as well to Paul and Carolyn Mancuso, who openly shared their own stories as well as their stories about Maureen.

It was a great pleasure to speak with Sheila, Carol, and Jo-Ann, Maureen's teammates at the North York Track Club. They are revolutionaries in their own right, each with a story worthy of its own book. Their reconnection during this project has been a joy to watch.

More than ten years ago, John Chipman uncovered Moe's story and tracked down Moe herself, then working as a professional dog groomer. His journalism reunited Moe with Kathrine and as Moe likes to say, "Finally gave me my moment." Thanks to John for his excellent reporting and for rehashing how he found Moe for our story.

Thanks to Kathrine for all of her help with this project, for sharing her memories of the fast little girl with the Monkees picture, and of course, for her tireless work in fighting for equality in sport for women. Thanks also to Des, whose running is an inspiration to people all over the world today. Her support for her teammates and her incredible performances will power the next generation of runners.

We contacted many sources who made brief appearances or were not directly referenced in this book but provided invaluable information to help complete the story, including Johnathan Reeves, Patti Ford-Bisborrow, Roberta Picco, Amby Burfoot, Robert Moore, Doug Smith, Lynn Borque, Rico Maideras, and Steve Price, who lent us his archive of the amazing magazine, *Cinderbellas*—an invaluable snapshot of the world of women's running in the 1960s. Thank you also to Gord Sim, who passed away but left us with a wonderful poem about Moe's marathon.

This book started as an episode of the *Human Race* podcast for *Runner's World*. Thank you to David Willey, Christine Fennessy, Brian Dalek, and Sylvia Ryerson, who gave great feedback and guidance on our original story.

We'd also like to thank our amazing editor Wes Adams, who gave us insightful edits and a runner's deep knowledge, and perhaps more importantly, was rather patient with our definition of deadlines. And thank you to our wonderful agent, Mackenzie Brady Watson, whose guidance and support helped make this book possible.

Kit: I would like to thank my original editors in life, Mom and Pops. And my ever-patient girlfriend, who sacrificed many dates to watch me pull my hair out in front of a computer screen in the final weeks.

Rachel: I would like to thank my husband, Tim. His tireless support and frequent evangelizing about this project and my work is a gift. My parents, like Moe's, sacrificed an enormous amount to give me opportunities. Their support is central to every success today.

INDEX